Chick

Indian Doctor's Soul.

Chicken Soup for the Indian Doctor's Soul

101 Inspirational and Uplifting Stories of Healing

**Jack Canfield,
Mark Victor Hansen,
Raksha Bharadia**

westland

We would like to acknowledge the following publishers and individuals for permission to reprint the following material. (Note: the stories that were penned anonymously or that are public domain are not included in this listing.)

A Stitch in Time. Reprinted by permission of Smita Shenoy. © 2011 Smita Shenoy.

Flying High. Reprinted by permission of Shifa Maitra. © 2011 Shifa Maitra.

His First Patient. Reprinted by permission of Aarti K. Pathak. © 2011 Aarti K. Pathak.

(continued on page 359)

westland ltd
Venkat Towers, 165, P.H. Road, Maduravoyal, Chennai 600 095
No. 38/10 (New No. 5), Raghava Nagar, New Timber Yard Layout, Bangalore 560 026
Survey No. A-9, II Floor, Moula Ali Industrial Area, Moula Ali, Hyderabad 500 040
23/181, Anand Nagar, Nehru Road, Santacruz East, Mumbai 400 055
4322/3, Ansari Road, Daryaganj, New Delhi 110 002

Copyright © 2011 Chicken Soup for the Soul Publishing LLC

All rights reserved

10 9 8 7 6 5 4 3 2 1

ISBN: 978-93-80658-66-7

This edition is published under arrangement with Chicken Soup for the Soul Publishing LLC, its logos and marks are trademarks of Chicken Soup for the Soul Publishing LLC

This edition is for sale in India, Pakistan, Bangladesh, Nepal and Sri Lanka only

Cover photograph courtesy Corbis Images

Inside book formatting and typesetting by Ram Das Lal

Printed at Aegean Offset Printers, Greater Noida

This book is sold subject to the condition that it shall not by way of trade or otherwise, be lent, resold, hired out, circulated, and no reproduction in any form, in whole or in part (except for brief quotations in critical articles or reviews) may be made without written permission of the publishers.

Contents

13. ON GRATITUDE

Introduction

She was all of one-and-a-half years old. Two nurses were holding her down while a third was trying to insert a syringe into a vein to get a blood sample. She was crying loudly, but I was crying even louder. We had no option. It was the fifth day and the fever had not broken; it was imperative that we run the test to rule out typhoid. They finally asked me to leave the room, not just because they were embarrassed at a grown-up crying, but because they thought it would be easier and quicker for the child if the mother was not in the room. They got her out within a few minutes. She jumped into my arms and gave a few more loud wails. Fresh tears streamed down my eyes as we made our way out of the wretched pathology lab. Her paediatrician was getting into the building just then. Between sobs I told him how my daughter had flung the syringe and the lab had to have three attendants on her to collect the sample. As I was talking, my voice broke (happens to first-time moms☺). To my surprise, Dr Patel handed me his briefcase and stethoscope, took my girl in his arms and went to the store just a few paces away. He bought her a Cadbury bar and my daughter's face lit up like a million bucks. Gone were the tears, the memory of the syringe, smell of antiseptic, cotton ... everything receded to the background as she unwrapped the big bar with her tiny fingers and dug into it with all her heart. I smiled as the angelic doctor handed me my princess.

Welcome to *Chicken Soup for the Soul: Indian Doctors*, and an extraordinary world that is a whirlwind of triumphs, tragedies, challenges and an assortment of emotions. For centuries, doctors have been amongst the most respected members of society, revered for their knowledge of the healing arts. For obvious reasons, we cannot help the ambivalence in our feelings towards them. As much as we may try to, no amount of apples can keep the doctors away and they become an integral part of our lives. Our contributing authors have generously opened their hearts, sharing their personal experiences with doctors who have either changed their lives radically or made a noteworthy difference to it. We also have numerous stories from doctors that enlighten us about their thoughts, outlook and everyday life, something that has always been obscure for us.

We bring to you stories of how doctors, in the eyes of their patients, transcend humanity, rising to a standing that is close to God's. Interestingly, we also have incidents from doctors, who have revealed that exulting in the glory of playing God is always a fleeting experience, because He definitely has His own ways of reminding them that they are merely human, and ensuring that they have their feet firmly established on the ground.

Some doctor-patient relationships start as a professional association and grow with time, over regular consultations as well as other shared experiences such as childbirth, hospitalisation and home visits, developing into a beautiful and strong bond. This rapport is based on understanding, faith and compassion. The attachment soon becomes deep and many times doctors find themselves donning several hats — of physician, friend, guide, mentor and saviour. We have heartrending stories of doctors going that extra mile to help their patients deal with a looming tragedy and sometimes even shedding tears with them. And these tales certainly put the common belief to rest that doctors are devoid of emotions when it comes to patients. Several of our stories from doctors reveal that the amiability in these relationships is mutual. The gratitude, faith and love that they get in return for their services goes a long way in shaping their individuality. It is a wonderful feeling to be on the receiving end of such profound affection. Each interaction with patients is also a valuable spring of learning for doctors who are constantly looking for remedies and respite in this vicious world of stress, disease and heartbreak.

We have some sweet and amusing stories from our contributing authors describing their comical trysts with the medical world, bringing to light the sunny side of doctors' temperaments, usually presumed to be grave and brusque. Yes, they do have a sense of humour too!

We have anecdotes that lend credence to the conviction that healing is not just a science, it is an art. In these stories you will see how when medicines alone fail to have the desired effect, doctors work on the vulnerable minds of the patients, instilling

in them positive thoughts and the will to live. We have some
soul-stirring stories of doctors and patients praying together
for a miracle during moments of hopelessness ... and miracles
have happened. As you read these stories you will share
the sorrow and the happiness that comes with each process
of healing. Our doctors live a life where they are constantly
stretching their limits and give all they can in terms of support
and care. They work round the clock tirelessly, making instant
decisions that could mean the difference between life and
death. If they silently celebrate their triumphs, they silently
mourn our tragedies as well.

So, dear reader, if you are all 'scrubbed' up by now, get ready
to venture into the fascinating world of medicine, doctors and
patients through this wonderful collection of 101 stories. And
if any of the stories feel familiar and make you want to put
down your own experiences, do so and share it with us!

Raksha Bharadia

1

SAVING LIVES

In nothing do men more nearly approach the gods than in giving health to men.

—Cicero

A Stitch in Time

My determination to give birth to my first-born in my hometown was not deterred by the fact that it was more of a village. Leaving the comforts of my home in the buzzing metropolis, I made my way to our ancestral house where I welcomed my daughter into this world amidst the serene surroundings.

A few sleepless nights later we were all wise to the saying 'it takes an entire village to raise a child'. How a mere infant could keep all the fourteen members of the household on their toes is a subject worthy of research!

My post pregnancy body demanded rest while my child commanded attention. Trying to keep both of them happy left me perpetually tired and woefully short of sleep. On that fateful night, as I was nursing my daughter, I dozed off. Sometime later, a horrible choking sound woke me up. Instinctively I looked at my daughter and realised what had happened; milk had probably gone into her windpipe!

As she struggled for breath I watched stunned. I summoned the strength and screamed my lungs out. Instantly the entire household had gathered in my room. For a minute their reactions mirrored mine — shock and helplessness. It was 3 a.m., dead of the night, and the nearest hospital was twenty-five kilometres away.

All eyes turned to me and I was chastised for being a 'careless' mother, etc. And I knew I deserved every single epithet that was coming my way.

All of a sudden my aunt swung into action. She picked up the infant and ran nearly two kilometres, to her daughter's paediatrician, Dr Labba's house. She kept on ringing the bell till the doctor opened the door, groggy eyed and dishevelled. One look at the infant, and he immediately grasped the situation. He guided my aunt to the clinic behind his house where she laid the baby on the small cot. He took out a small pump-like device from the cupboard and got down to work.

By this time my daughter had almost turned blue. Even the choking sounds she had been making had stopped. His face grim, he kept sucking out the milk from her nose in small quantities. Three minutes passed but there was no change. Five minutes later, there was still no change. My aunt was in tears but the doctor carried on relentlessly. Suddenly, the room was filled with the sounds of my baby's cries, and the colour slowly returned to her face.

The doctor, who had been holding his breath for so long, heaved a sigh of relief. 'Everything is fine,' he said, yet the three words were charged with inexplicable emotions.

He refused to accept any fees, saying he had merely done his duty. He dropped my aunt and baby back home in his car and came in to assure us that everything was fine.

Dr Labba looked at me standing in the corner of the room,

a mixture of guilt and relief on my face. He came and stood beside me.

'I know what you are going through but please understand this is not your fault,' he said in his kindest voice. 'You are no superwoman. Becoming a mother does not mean neglecting your health and your needs. Childbirth is a massive process and the body needs special care. You have to give it that. Your child will be looked after by your family members but your body has to be nurtured only by you. Adequate sleep is essential during this time. Do not compromise on that, especially when you have so many loving, helping hands around.'

After a pause he continued. 'An innocent one suffered terribly for no fault of hers. If the milk had reached her lungs she could have developed pneumonia. And I think you understand how grave the situation could have become.'

A collective shudder went through the room; yes, we could understand and we could not thank god enough for my aunt's presence of mind and the doctor's prompt actions.

Even now whenever I visit my hometown, my aunt narrates the incident. She weaves the incident into a moving tale with a happy ending as I hang on to her words with childlike enthusiasm. She always ends the narration thus: 'Thank god for selfless and dedicated doctors. May their tribe grow!'

Amen.

Smita Shenoy

Flying High

I had a long day and was travelling back on a midnight flight. All I needed was some peace and quiet to rest and catch up on my sleep. As soon as I had settled in, I noticed a mousy looking man sitting next to me. He was fidgety and kept shifting in his seat. A nervous flyer was all I needed for company, I thought warily. While I tried to unwind I was beginning to get irritated with this nerd.

On the seat behind me was a woman who was snoring and wheezing all at the same time. Her two teenage daughters were talking nonstop about their clothing for a wedding they were going to attend in Bangkok. So much for sleep, I thought. The cabin lights were dimmed and I could hear the nerd next to me typing away on his laptop. Being a light sleeper is not easy .... Suddenly there was a sound that could rouse the devil out of his stupor. The woman in the back seat seemed to be having a heart attack.

The cabin crew rushed to her, and the lights came on. Her daughters were hysterical. The pilot made an announcement asking if there was a doctor on board. There was stunned silence — I couldn't take my eyes off the lady who seemed to be hovering between life and death.

Suddenly the nerd in the next seat got up, and I was shocked. Dentists are doctors too, he said and went to help the lady. He then asked everyone to move away, made her lie down and asked the airhostess to get the medicine box. Next he spoke to the captain and as they were in a huddle, the rest of us were clueless as to what was happening.

Suddenly his personality changed, he was in charge and in command. With the captain next to him, he said she needed prayers but the immediate danger was taken care of, adding that the sooner she got medical aid, the better it was for her. There was a collective sigh of relief. The captain announced that we were making an emergency landing in Nagpur and the flight would be delayed.

I saw an elderly man across the aisle taking out his prayer beads. When I went to the rest room, I saw an adorable little child with his eyes closed and hands folded, praying earnestly. Seeing this, my faith in humanity was restored.

Back on my seat I kept observing this miracle worker who was cradling the lady's head in his lap and talking to her like she was a child. He gestured to me and asked me to tell the daughters to calm down and talk to their mom. He said that she had to stay awake and keep on talking, and if she didn't, the chances of her slipping into a coma were high.

Soon I was watching from a distance as the two daughters and the good doctor were rubbing her palms, the soles of her feet and talking to her, telling her stories of the wonderful times in the past ... and their plans for the future. Her pulse rate was returning to normal. Her breathing was getting even. The prayers of 270-odd people seemed to be working.

On touchdown in Nagpur, like the movies, there were ambulances and cops on the tarmac. Paramedics rushed in and she was gently lifted onto a stretcher. The dentist went along till the ambulance. I saw him on the tarmac as the ambulance sped away.

When he boarded the plane again, he was met with a standing ovation. The captain shook his hand and said that he was so glad to have him — Dr Rao — on his flight. And I swore never to go by first impressions again!

Shifa Maitra

His First Patient

Dr Amit had just completed his internship at the local government hospital and was delighted when he was selected to work in that very same hospital. It was his first day at work as a qualified doctor, and he planned to reach the hospital well before the scheduled time of 9 a.m.

At about the time, in another part of the city, a young woman was hurrying to work. Her gait was awkward as she was in an advanced stage of pregnancy but that did not prevent her from attempting to keep up with the fast pace of movement around her. Suddenly, she lost her balance and fell face down on the pavement. A jagged metal piece lying there caused a severe gash right through her stomach.

'My baby, my baby!' she screamed in pain and fear, holding on to her blood-drenched stomach in a protective gesture. The people around her stopped momentarily and then moved on, but not everyone. A kind stranger ran into her house in the nearby slum and brought out a worn sheet, quickly wrapped it around the bleeding woman's abdomen in a desperate attempt to contain the flow of blood, and then carried her to a taxi which agreed to take them to a hospital.

When Dr Amit reached the hospital, he found the reception area in a state of turmoil. A nurse informed him that an injured woman in an advanced stage of pregnancy had been brought in. 'Dr Prakash and Dr Suman cannot take on this case; they are attending to other seriously ill patients. She is slipping fast!' said the nurse. 'I don't think she will hold on much longer.'

Dr Amit moved swiftly to the patient who had by now been placed on a stretcher. 'Take her to the OT; I will operate on her immediately.' The quiet resolve in his voice surprised the nurses and attendants and they moved promptly to carry out his orders. An hour later, the doctor came out of the OT. The woman had lost a lot of blood but she would live; but the miracle was that she had given birth to a healthy baby boy.

Later in the day, the senior doctor in charge called Dr Amit and complimented him for his dedication and skill. But then he asked, 'Amit, most young doctors prefer to start their careers with straightforward cases that guarantee success. This lady could most likely have died on your operating table. This being your first day, what made you take this bold decision?'

'Sir, after I had operated on the patient, I met the woman who had brought her to the hospital. A total stranger, she had hurried and tied a sheet around the patient to stem the loss of blood. I also spoke to the taxi driver who had given up his daily wage to help. I asked them why they did what they did for someone they did not even know. Their answer was simple yet revealing. They said that they could not stand and watch when someone so desperately needed help. I think I too felt the same. A part of me said that it was a hopeless case, but I felt that I could not let her die, without even trying to help. I had to fight for that slim chance, even though the odds were stacked against her.'

When Dr Amit left, the senior doctor remained in a contemplative mood. He had seen a very special force in action today, a force more powerful than any medical skill; one that was created by faith and selflessness and that force had created a miracle which he had been privileged to witness.

The woman saved by Dr Amit that fateful day, a humble domestic servant named Kusum, resides happily in Mumbai with her family. The baby boy saved that day is now in college. He has two younger siblings as well.

Aarti K. Pathak

Matter of Life and Death

As a plastic surgeon, I handle many different types of cases. Sometimes, the patient seeks correctional surgery for personal reasons, sometimes for professional reasons and at other times, for pain relief. The motivation for cosmetic surgery varies depending on the patient's age and social situation. A plastic surgeon's work can dramatically improve a patient's quality of life. For those, like me, who belong to this group of medical practitioners, the most gratifying part of our job is when we are able to restore form and function in its true and complete sense.

Swati, a young mother of two, was in the puja room of her home trying to distract the baby with the assorted bells and idols on the shelves, when disaster struck. The loose folds of her nightgown brushed against a lit oil lamp and burst into flames, enveloping her. The only other person at home then was her other son, a seven-year-old. The little boy somehow managed to get his baby brother out of the room and call for help. Swati was rushed to hospital where her condition, although serious, appeared stable, at least for the initial two weeks.

All of a sudden, however, things took a turn for the worse and she began fighting for her life. We had to shift her to the ICU where her situation continued to be critical. She was brought in with about fifty per cent burns and this made me realise that I had taken on a case that was beyond my capacity. I felt she should be moved to another hospital where they were better equipped to deal with burn cases.

I called a medical college in Bangalore and they asked me to shift the patient to their facility. However, Swati's family would have none of this — they refused to shift her to another hospital and insisted that I treat her, irrespective of the end result. They stood by me with full confidence.

It was a tough situation to be in. I was filled with misgivings but I also had to make sure the family didn't lose confidence. I decided to do a root cause analysis to uncover all the factors that could have caused her to deteriorate so suddenly. I soon hit upon one major contributing factor — although the nutritionist had put Swati on a high protein diet, she was not consuming any of it. At the end of the day, housekeeping would pick up her largely untouched tray and cart it away. A burn patient requires three to four times more protein than the average person in order to rebuild burnt skin tissues and preserve immunity. Devoid of the essential key nutrients, Swati's condition had worsened rapidly.

Her refusal to eat was largely spurred by maternal separation pangs — she was missing her baby. Having found the root cause for her critical condition, I counselled her, citing the cause for her deterioration and the importance of nutrition for a quick recovery to enable her to return to her baby at the earliest. That counselling had its intended effect; she changed her attitude and cooperated with the hospital staff. Her recovery progressed well from that point on and she was soon out of the hospital. Within a month and without any further surgical intervention, she had recovered almost completely.

With the mounting cost of hospitalisation, the family had reached its financial limits and we had to discharge her. This was not such a bad thing, in my view, as the risk of infection for someone in her vulnerable condition was higher in a hospital setting. I thought I would allow her wounds to improve to become suitable for skin graft procedure and then readmit her for the procedure. As it turned out, I didn't need to do this. With a nutritious diet and capable nursing help at home, Swati was soon on her feet and didn't require any other surgical procedures.

Last year, I got a call from her. She wanted me to know that she was preparing for the Karnataka Administrative Service (KAS) exam and asked for my blessing. I asked her why she had set herself that particular goal. She answered, 'I got a second chance in life and I don't want to waste it. I want to prove to myself that I can do it.' Swati hasn't passed the exam as yet but that is not stopping her from continuing to try. There is a stronger sense of purpose in her now. She has clarity of vision that only someone who has hovered between life and death can probably have.

As told to Shashi Agarwal

The Doctor of Champawat

Life couldn't have been more promising for Dr Pramod Karnatic. He had just completed his MS from S.N. Medical College, Agra, and was awarded a gold medal for his exemplary performance.

Enthusiastic and idealistic, the doctor was raring to go. He chose one of the reputed hospitals in Mumbai for his practice. He had an insatiable appetite for learning and there was an ocean of knowledge out there. But within six months the young doctor found himself battling his broken illusions. The red-tape and commercialisation consumed all his glorious principles of service. He felt claustrophobic and stifled. During this time there came an opportunity for him to join as a surgeon in the Primary Health Centre in the small village of Champawat in the interiors of Kumaon, Uttarakhand. He agreed.

Champawat was extremely backward and famous for its man-eating tigers. Dr Pramod reached there and realised that it was truly the back of the beyond. No doctor had ever worked there in the past and people actually relied on spirits and ghosts to cure their illnesses.

The bright enthusiastic doctor got a small room for his clinic, with a table and a chair. The local quacks were hostile and were waiting for the so-called highly qualified doctor to either run away or join their lackadaisical ways.

But Dr Pramod was a determined soul. He worked hard in the primitive conditions. At first the villagers were wary of him and kept their distance, but soon they started warming up to him. From high fevers and burns to fractures, he was tested in his capabilities and knowledge.

One day, a group of villagers came running to him in absolute panic. A twelve-year-old Nepali boy had been stabbed brutally in his abdomen by a lunatic. Dr Pramod rushed to find the boy lying in a pool of blood, barely breathing. The doctor knew that the odds were stacked against him, but the internal bleeding had to be stopped.

The boy was taken to his clinic where Dr Pramod rolled up his sleeves and set out to cut open the abdomen. Once opened, he saw a big gash in the liver; to stitch it up he would need to cut open the chest too, but there was no anaesthesia. With the help of sedatives and his determination, Dr Pramod went on with his task. The chest was opened, sutures were applied deftly and neatly and everything was put back together again.

It was a tough call. There was pin drop silence as the villagers peeped through the window incredulously, with a deep sense of awe and gratitude. The doctor sat through the night as the boy's breathing slowly resumed to normal. The colour came back to his face and he was at last out of danger. After a month of medication and rest, the boy was back on his feet.

The doctor had finally arrived. He was embraced by the simple people of Champawat as their saviour, which the doctor proved to be time and again — operating under candle light, stove light, on the cot, on a bench, or even on a pile of bricks — wherever, however, with or without anaesthesia. More often than not he found himself taking care of those who had been mauled by bears and panthers. Once he had a patient whose stomach had been ripped open by a bull. He removed tumours, healed tuberculosis patients, cured alcoholics and even delivered babies. The doctor was a neurosurgeon, paediatrician, orthopaedist, gynaecologist, urologist, cardiologist ... he was all in one.

Over time Champawat became a district; government health care received a boost but with it came a whole lot of bureaucratic complications and the doctor found himself getting sucked into a vortex of paperwork, and soon, distanced from those who needed him.

That is when he decided to leave the comforts of the government job and geared up to start a small hospital on his own. There was a scarcity of funds and facilities, but he used every possible resource. His new bride too proved to be his true soulmate and willingly gave up all her desires and dreams of a rosy life for his mission, helping him in every way she could. His fees, for those who could afford it, was a meagre Rs 10, and he charged Rs 50 for surgeries, but for most of the villagers even that was waived off for an odd pumpkin or melon from their farm or even a grateful smile.

Mr Peter Brickbac, an Anglo-Ceylonese missionary, was so moved by Dr Pramod's commitment and selflessness that he gave him a large piece of land.

And thus the doctor's journey went on and the saga continues till today. It proves how a caring heart and pure dedication can make all the difference in the world and give rise to waterfalls in a desert.

Archna Pant

The Pact

I was just about to leave my clinic when I received a telephone call from Udaipur saying that a seriously ill child was being brought to me. The child, accompanied by his grandfather, was indeed very ill and had to be admitted to the hospital and placed on a ventilator.

The child stayed in the hospital for almost two months with very little improvement in his condition. But children are often very resilient, and so I kept giving hope to the parents and to the grandfather. One day, the grandfather told me that it was imperative for him to go back to Udaipur. He had to look after the family business as there was no one else in charge there. The parents would stay behind.

The grandfather had hardly been gone a week when we received news that he had passed away. Within days of his demise, the child, who had been struggling for months to survive, began to make a rapid recovery. In a few weeks, he was well enough to be discharged and sent home.

I remember how proud and happy the parents were when they brought him to me with his first school report card. Seeing him so healthy and normal, it would have been difficult for anyone to imagine that just six months ago he had been so gravely ill.

Now, I am a rational person. I am sure that the grandfather must have had a lot of health problems and the added stress of his grandchild's illness hastened his death. I know that it was the cumulative effect of the hospital care and the treatment that had got the child out of his prolonged illness.

But sometimes I wonder ... is it possible that the grandfather could have made a pact with God? A pact that took the grandfather's life but let a little boy live?

Dr Ajit

2

BONDING WITH PATIENTS

Body and soul cannot be separated for purposes of treatment, for they are one and indivisible. Sick minds must be healed as well as sick bodies.

–C. Jeff Miller

Amma and Doctor Uttam

'Make a call to Uttam. I've had this irritating cough for a week now and nothing seems to help,' said my nonagenarian mother.

'But Amma, Dr Uttam is an orthopaedic surgeon. I think you need to consult a physician.'

'No!' My mother is adamant. 'Uttam understands my problems well. He's the only doctor I can trust.'

Amma met Dr Uttam Vaish over a decade ago when she had a bout of severe osteoarthritic pain. She took to the young, gentle and soft-spoken doctor who seemed to have all the time in the world to listen to every detail of her aches and pains. Besides, he resembled her younger son a lot and the two bonded quite well.

Amma swore by Dr Uttam's treatment and soon more than half of her extended family was consulting him for their orthopaedic problems. Tasnim's father-in-law, another nonagenarian, had a hip joint replacement and was able to walk soon after the surgery. Taha, my nephew, fractured his ankle on the very first day of the Board examinations but thanks to

Dr Uttam, he didn't have to miss a single paper. The entire Ali clan headed for Dr Uttam's clinic for all sorts of problems, from sprained ankles, pulled ligaments, compressed sciatica, slipped disc, lumbago, frozen shoulders, to cracked ribs and a variety of skeletal disorders.

And we weren't the only ones. His clinic was always crowded with patients of all ages willing to wait for as long as it took simply because it was worth the wait. When you have an elbow dislocation or a stiff neck, a sympathetic smile and kind words of reassurance from the doctor help as much as the medical treatment.

Amma, of course, had expectations much beyond Dr Uttam's line of specialisation. She consulted him for oral ulcers, stomach disorders and skin allergies. Dr Uttam always prescribed some medicine, which my mother felt worked miracles for her. The only time he gently declined from treating her was when she wanted him to correct a root canal problem.

One day Amma called Dr Uttam, and their conversation went thus:

'My pet cat Chhotu is very listless these days. He won't eat his food, walks with a limp and seems to be in great pain.'

I saw her nodding into the receiver and then writing something on the notepad.

'Uttam says give Chhotu half a digene tablet and a quarter tablet of disprin dissolved in water,' she informed me after putting down the phone.

And sure enough Chhotu recovered completely after just one dose and Amma was elated.

'You are an angel in disguise, beta, a true doctor with a heart of gold,' she told Dr Uttam that evening. 'May you excel in your profession and may God give you a long, happy and prosperous life with your loved ones.'

And so it went on that way with Amma and Dr Uttam. It was a symbiotic relationship; he lent her his ear, patience and consideration and she in turn wished him well and blessed him as she would her son.

Rehana Ali

Being a Chocolate Boy

I have visited many physicians in my twenty odd years, so I was shocked when my father told me that he had always gone to the same doctor from his childhood till he turned forty. He stopped visiting the doctor only after the old man passed away.

'See, back in our days, everybody went to their neighbourhood doctor for everything. Be it for common cold, diarrhoea or even something major like gall bladder stones,' my father stated matter-of-factly.

'But I'm sure they had specialists and good clinics in the city then, right?' I asked.

'Yes, there were some when I was a bit older, but I didn't need to see a fancy degree or an air-conditioned clinic to get good medical care. Dr Sarkar was a part of my life from day one,' my father explained.

Then he went on to tell me about a couple of incidents that made me realise why my father had kept on returning to Dr Sarkar and his cramped, hot chamber in the narrow lane.

One day when my father had fallen down while playing a game of football on the streets, my grandfather had taken him to Dr Sarkar for first aid and to ensure that no bones were broken. It turned out that everything was fine but my father's ego had taken a hit, because the older boys playing with him had laughed loudly at his fall.

So he kept on crying and that worried the doctor and my grandfather until finally my father blurted out the reason.

'They said I should play dolls with the girls!'

While my grandfather had looked uncomfortable, the doctor had sat next to my father and talked to him about bullies and explained the saying, 'sticks and stones will break my bones but mean words won't hurt me'. To this day, my father mutters this phrase when the situation requires it, as I do too, since childhood.

A few years after that, my father had developed a sweet tooth that was getting to be an issue for his health. He had numerous sessions with the doctor where healthy eating and exercise were discussed. No diet charts were made. They had discussions where my grandfather voiced his concern but the patient wasn't given any lecture.

So finally a deal was reached — Dr Sarkar would allow my grandfather to give my father a small bar of chocolate every Sunday if the diet for the rest of the week was healthy. This plan worked well. Whenever my father would visit the chamber, Dr Sarkar would ask, 'How is my little chocolate boy?'

One day, Dr Sarkar asked my grandfather to send my father to his chamber. He had just returned from a trip to Europe and had brought some chocolate bars for my father. My father thanked him and promised to have it only once a week.

My father kept his promise and, till his death, Dr Sarkar would always bring chocolate for my father whenever he went abroad on a trip. And not caring that he was now quite a bit older than the start of the chocolate tradition, my father would have one every Sunday.

I have had nice doctors. I have had doctors who have successfully treated me. But this kind of bond, I've never even come close to it.

Sue Ghosh

Both a Mother and a Doctor

'I'd like to speak to the doctor ... please tell her that this is the same Lakshmi who still cries for her mother ....'

Of all the calls I'd taken for my doctor parents, this was undoubtedly the strangest. There have been patients who'd identify themselves with their complaints tagged on as suffixes to their names, but this strange identification was certainly a first. I duly passed the message to my mother, and sure enough, she did recognise this particular Lakshmi from her other namesakes on her patients' list. The call was hush-hush with the requisite doctor-patient confidentiality, but my incessant wheedling made my mother open up just a little on this particular patient's history.

'She comes to me for psoriasis treatment ... very tough, you know,' said my mother. I did know. Psoriasis was one of the more dreaded diseases in my mother's repertoire — as a dermatologist, she was subjected to a daily dose of acne, dry skin and dark spots, but there were the occasional more serious complications. And psoriasis was one of them — a hereditary disease that suppresses the immune system, and hastens the skin's life cycle, leaving unsightly patches of flaky white and red skin in its wake.

In fact, my mother would insist that her role was more of a counsellor than a dermatologist, advising her patients on coping with the disease that had the dubious distinction of rarely going into remission and progressively worsening over time.

But her relationship with Lakshmi had been on a strictly professional basis, until the patient had come to my mother's clinic some time ago with a sudden outbreak of symptoms. The medications had been fixed upon after much trial and error, and the disease had been finally brought under control. Lakshmi's case was considered to belong to a more subdued category … but yet she'd turned up with a renewed outbreak of peeling skin on her arms, face and torso. The baffled doctor had asked if she was under any kind of stress, and the response had been startlingly dramatic. Lakshmi, bursting into tears, had sobbed, 'My mummy died … I miss her so much … I don't know how I'll live without my mummy ….'

'I spoke to her for over twenty minutes,' said my mother. 'She still comes in every week, even if there's no progress or problem with her disease. She just comes to talk; she's devastated and doesn't know how to cope. She's visiting a psychiatrist, but still …' I could hear the sympathy mixed with something like affinity in my mother's voice.

And there was no need for me to ask her about Lakshmi's introduction that day, or to wonder just why a lady of fifty was grieving so heartbrokenly for her 'mummy'. There was no need for me to figure what she was getting out of her weekly visits, or why my mother found Lakshmi's case so compelling that she set aside entire half-an-hour slots for this patient. My mother was a lady of fifty too, with grandchildren of her own, and she'd never stopped grieving for her own mother, a whole decade after her death.

Over the years, my mother graduated from being Lakshmi's doctor to her philosopher and guide. Lakshmi would come in for consultation on topics varying from her condition to her daughter's marriage. My mother advised Lakshmi on how to camouflage her condition and how to control the stress that would in all certainty lead to fresh outbreak. She comforted her patient on the dreadful day when Lakshmi's daughter broke out into rashes that looked horribly like psoriasis, and rejoiced with them when it turned out to be a harmless allergy. She advised Lakshmi to be frank when she wanted to know how to deal with a prospective alliance for her daughter.

My mother was also regretfully honest with the groom's family when they visited her, saying, 'Yes, the condition could be hereditary, but there's no reason to suppose your grandchild will be afflicted too. Having said that, there are plenty of ways to control the disease … they're a lovely family, and your son couldn't do better…', and almost got into a fistfight when they were not convinced by her repeated assurances that Lakshmi's condition was not contagious.

She rushed to the ER when Lakshmi's husband desperately called one night, telling her that his wife had taken an overdose of pills. She stayed with the family, waiting until Lakshmi was out of danger, and finally woke up to say, 'I just cannot go on without my mother, I want to join her'. She gave the sheepish patient a sharp dose of common sense, and rushed to her own hospital at noon, doling out advice on acne treatment and skin lightening creams, while all the time fretting about Lakshmi's exploit, and her condition, which had reached an unprecedented level with the stress of the suicide attempt.

She talked at length with the psychiatrist, and figured out how best to help Lakshmi snap out of her morbid state. She helped her patient's sorrow transit from the initial stabbing pain, into a more constant and a livable ache; showing her that life could go on inspite of the crippling loss of an understanding parent. And she showed Lakshmi, and me too, that under the cool and business-like pose of a competent doctor, there lies an individual whose hopes and pains can be very much similar to the patients they treat. The long exposure to pain and suffering might have perhaps hardened into a veneer of professional apathy, but sometimes their professional masks slip in the face of affinity with a similarly suffering patient, and they transcend the boundaries of doctor-patient relationship into a more personal and mutually comforting level.

Lakshmi still calls — for she still grieves for her mother. I suspect that whenever she feels her loss too hard to bear, she calls up my mother, identifying herself as 'the motherless Lakshmi'. And I know that my mother will put aside her work for a while to comfort her, both as a doctor, and as a fellow motherless daughter.

Gayathri Ponvannan

Doctor Babu

It was after six years of marriage that Bulbul Aunty was expecting. As the news of her pregnancy spread, everyone recommended some or the other gynaecologist who was supposed to have a miraculous touch, and had done wonders with the most complex of cases.

However, Bulbul Aunty stuck to her 'Doctor Babu'. He was not a gynaecologist but a member of the Royal Colleges of Physicians, UK. This eighty-something physician never required any tests to understand what was wrong with a patient. He would read the pulse of the patient and that was enough for him to detect the cause, the effect and the cure of the illness. However, my aunt's faith in Doctor Babu was not accepted easily by many of her 'well-wishers'.

'What kind of a doctor is he? It's been four months now, and he still hasn't asked for any ultrasound.'

'Your monthly expenses are so low? Are you sure about this doctor?'

'He must be crazy for having allowed you to go to Kedarnath in the third month. You should change your doctor immediately!'

My aunt was getting used to the uninvited concern from her 'well-wishers' and she would smartly turn a deaf ear to them.

The couple had immense faith in their physician. They had known him for about four years now. Their meeting was quite interesting in itself. My uncle and aunt had been returning home on their scooter when suddenly a dog ran into the middle of the street. My uncle swerved to the left to save the poor animal and accidently hit an old man carrying a bag full of vegetables. Thankfully, the old man was alright, but my aunt seemed to have sprained her ankle and couldn't move. The old man helped my uncle to move Bulbul Aunty into his house, which was nearby.

'I am from here, but I have never seen you before,' my uncle said, after apologising again for having scattered his vegetables and crushing the eggs.

'Well, I shifted to this place just a week back.'

'I see. Where are you from, Sir?'

'London.'

'London must be great. What do you do there?'

'Well, I just help people to get rid of their illnesses,' he said, as he pulled out a spray from a broken wooden cupboard. Bulbul Aunty was by now crying in pain; she was least interested in the conversation. However, the spray didn't take long to soothe her pain.

'Let me arrange for a rickshaw. We will get an X-ray done in the evening,' my uncle announced as he got up.

'X-ray?' exclaimed the doctor. 'Your wife is absolutely fine. In fact, I would suggest that she walks. Your house is a short distance from here, and there is nothing like an evening walk in this weather.'

'Are you sure, Doctor? Actually, she is a little fragile.'

The doctor laughed his lungs out at my uncle's statement. 'We humans are the strongest of all the species, and are the chosen ones to take care of the Almighty's creations. But we have made ourselves the weakest of all. Your wife is fine, she doesn't need any further treatment,' he declared.

My cousin was born healthy without any costly consultation or expensive medicines. My aunt was able to have a normal delivery. All she did were a few exercises suggested by Doctor Babu.

My cousin Akki was growing up under the guidance of his 'Doctor Dadu'. Unlike other kids who were scared of doctors, Akki's visits were like a walk to the children's park. He would play with the stethoscope and write prescriptions in the notepad whenever he visited Doctor Dadu's chamber. Doctor Dadu would just take a look at him, put his palm on Akki's little forehead, and know exactly what was wrong with the little monster.

On Akki's fourth birthday, his parents took him on a ten-day trip to Manali. They enjoyed their vacation and got gifts for everyone. But apart from the toys, jackets and a muffler, Akki got himself a cold and a mild fever too. So my uncle took him to Doctor Dadu for a check-up. He was a little surprised to see the door locked.

'Arrey, Bose Babu! Where have you been all this while? We have all been trying to reach you,' a neighbour said on seeing my uncle.

'I had been on a vacation with my family. Where is Doctor Babu?'

'Bose Babu ... Doctor Babu expired last Thursday. He has left an envelope for you. Let me get it for you.' Saying this, the gentleman brought the letter and handed it over to my uncle.

Hands trembling, my uncle tore open the envelope to read the letter inside:

Hope you are enjoying your vacation. I am doing well too. But I am growing old, and old age comes with its own set of weaknesses. Some are curable, some are not. I am having some breathing problems. Even last year I had similar problems but I didn't give up. But I am not sure whether I will be able to make it this year.

I have been to Manali twice. With the kind of weather in that place during this time, I am sure Akki will come back with a running nose and an aching throat. Just give him a dose of Septran or Solvin twice a day for a week and he will be fine. I hope he will like the taste. That's all for now.

Take good care of yourself.

Yours,

Doctor Babu

Avantika Debnath

Dr Santa

The thermometer read 105.5 degrees. Obviously something was wrong with the reading, Janet thought and checked again after washing and re-setting the instrument. The same digits glared back at her.

Janet's five-year-old son Alex had come down with cough, cold and fever as he always did when the weather changed. It would linger for three to four days and then subside. But this time the fever was obstinate; it refused to go and kept on rising. Janet gave Alex a paracetamol and a quick sponge bath to bring down the fever. After an hour she checked — it was still 105 degrees.

'Don't worry. Bring him to the hospital now, let me take a look at him,' Dr Neena said calmly over the phone. Janet and her husband, Eric, rushed Alex to the hospital. Dr Neena examined his chest and then sent him for an X-ray. The procedure took fifteen minutes, and the result was apparent — Alex had chest congestion and Dr Neena suspected pneumonia. 'He needs to be hospitalised right away,' she announced.

'Mom, when will we shop for gifts and the tree? Christmas is only five days away. Can we please go home now?' Alex feebly asked his mother. He lay limp on the bed clad in a blue hospital gown, and was being administered medicines intravenously along with glucose. Janet felt like crying.

Slowly Alex showed signs of improvement. The fever was going down and his lungs seemed to be clearing out. Dr Neena was satisfied with his progress but the only thing she was unable to do was promise Alex that he would be going home before Christmas. Alex loved his paediatrician and had begun to believe that she was a magician, injecting magic potions into his body which would make him strong enough to get back home in time for Christmas. But every time he started his countdown, Dr Neena would force a smile and pat his head.

It was Christmas Eve and Alex had cried himself to sleep. He had refused to eat, or to take nebulisation or medicines. He felt certain now that he would not be going home today. His friends were all probably having a marvellous time while he was trapped here in this dreary hospital room at his favourite time of the year. Eric and Jane were heartbroken at their little boy's misery.

'Ho ho ho! Is Alex here? We've been looking everywhere for him!'

Alex rubbed his eyes in disbelief. A group of four strangely dressed people scuttled into his hospital room. And what had happened to his room? There was a beautiful little Christmas tree on a table and some colourful decorations on the windows. Red balloons were strewn on the floor. And who were these odd-looking people ... was it Dr Neena and her team from the children's ward?

Dr Neena was wearing a red jacket over her saree, a Santa's cap and had a white beard and moustache — crafted out of cotton wool — glued scruffily on her face. Her chubby build lent credence to her little Santa act; the two junior doctors and a nurse had painted their faces and were wearing peculiar hats, an unsuccessful but comical attempt at trying to look like Santa's elves!

They were carrying a tray of cookies glazed with multi-hued icing and sandwiches. Alex squealed with joy and almost jumped off his bed. He laughed and clapped his hands when two other children in hospital gowns were escorted in by a nurse, and then the party began.

The children gorged on the cookies and sandwiches and played with the balloons. Alex, Jane and Eric sang their favourite carols and everybody applauded enthusiastically. A junior doctor burst a confetti bomb giving an extra festive look to the room. The kids cheered ecstatically. After an hour of merry-making, Dr Neena announced that it was time to wrap up, and the children needed rest.

The room was cleaned up and order restored. Alex curled up in his bed with the remote-controlled car his parents had gifted him, and dozed off into a peaceful slumber. He was happy, content and exhausted.

When the doctors had started preparing for the little party, it was as much a surprise to Janet and Eric as it had been to Alex. Dr Neena's compassionate gesture had lit up the faces of the children and given Alex the most memorable Christmas of his life, when he had least expected it. Alex had been right — she was truly a magician who brought joy and cheer out of gloom.

When Dr Neena came in for her last round of the day, Alex's parents were at a loss for words. Tears of gratitude streamed down their faces and they could only say, 'Thank you, Doctor!' 'Ho ho ho,' replied Dr Neena and waddled out of the room.

Swati Rajgharia

Ria's Birthday

We were having dinner at a restaurant and Dr Uma smiled as the screen of her mobile phone flashed. The message read, 'She's tasted cake.' We cheered.

The birthday girl was one-year-old Ria who had already spent ten months in the Paediatric Intensive Care Unit (PICU) of a general hospital in Mumbai, on a ventilator. That meant she was unable to breathe on her own. If it weren't for those machines and medicines, she would be dead. If it weren't for the doctors, nurses, technicians, she'd be dead. For them, she was family, she was victory, she was one of the many dreams that have come true at that hospital, in that ward.

She had arrived underweight, in terrible distress both respiratory and otherwise. Her parents were drained of energy and finances, but not of the will to see her through whatever medical treatment that was required. Little mite, she had to be pricked and probed hundreds of times in order to see how she was functioning, to check which parts of her were functioning, to see what could be done to save her life. She couldn't inhale, she couldn't exhale. She was too weak and ill for that. No one thought she'd survive, but the doctors and nurses had a job to do and almost a year later, proved that they had done it well.

The day they'd arrived, Ria's father met another patient's father who told him his baby had been in that critical care ward for four months. It sounded like a terribly long time. Now, it appeared as if those ten months had passed in a jiffy. In those ten months, the nurses had grown terribly attached to the wonder girl who was responding, and who, after such a stretched and severe fight, was now ready to go home though still on the ventilator. The company that supplied the equipment had decided to waive off the rent for this infant who had made it, who was out of danger but not out of trouble yet. It was a kind gesture, an acknowledgment to the devotion of the staff at the hospital.

For a week there had been excitement in the ward — Ria's birthday was approaching. Ria was going to celebrate her birthday; it was like a miracle. Ria was the result of the combined efforts of brilliant minds, caring hands and technology. Ria was will-power personified, just a couple of kilos of her. Someone gifted streamers, someone gifted balloons, someone else gifted plastic flowers. Teddy-bears, squeaky toys, syringes, diapers, they all came gift-wrapped. So many frocks were received, from interns, registrars, staff nurses, student nurses, parents of other patients, ayahs....

The sick infant seemed happy as if she knew something was different around her. The machines she was hooked to were the same, the people were the same, but she sensed the activity, the laughter and cheer, the congratulations, the encouragement. Four times, no, five, or maybe even six times, her frock was

changed, and a new one put on every time. Crisp and colourful
— no hospital uniform for her on her special day.

   When the phone call came asking for permission to let
Ria taste a bit of cake, Dr Uma, the paediatrician I was with,
readily agreed. Cake in a PICU? Why not, she said, today's
a big day for everybody in the hospital. Ria's the 'person of
honour'; couldn't call her a guest, could she? Even her parents
had become a part of the hospital, for they ate and spent most
of their waking hours there. They took turns sleeping, with
the grandparents and other relatives. They were familiar with
all the workers, procedures, treatments. They had provided
solace to other parents, and had been a pillar of support for
anyone who needed it. They had understood the limitations of
modern medicine as well as its nearly magical 'powers'. They
knew well what it meant to have a child survive against every
single odd, that this was a landmark day for everyone, not just
for Ria or for them.

   It was a victory for the staff of that paediatric hospital that
was not flush with funds, where the poor of India flocked for the
best available treatment, where thousands of Mumbaikars of at
least four generations had been born, from whose portals had
walked out masters of their subject: paediatric care. Neonates
are like tadpoles, fragile and raw. They have to be tended with
utmost caution and delicate care. Those that handle them and
administer treatment have to be precise and unfailingly error-
free; the Rias of India owe such institutions a lot.

   With Dr Uma's approval, Ria received her first 'food', a mere
lick of cake. The claps that echoed through that PICU was
heard in the restaurant where we ate our dinner. Uma's eyes
shone — with victory, with affection, and with the satisfaction

that comes from a duty well done. She'd given so much to this baby, and the baby had come out of danger; well almost, for it was a long time before she'd be 'okay', but at least she was ready to go home.

The mobile phone was switched off, and a fresh thread of conversation started — of little babies who've battled illnesses at birth and lived to be adults. There's so much one can learn from doctors.

Sheela Jaywant

Erased

The scene is still vivid before my eyes even though it occurred eighteen years ago. As a young doctor, I had just started my practice as a paediatrician in a quiet and peaceful locality. Those were the early day of clinical practice and I was going through the endless waiting periods.

One rainy evening, two boys caught my attention as they came running into the clinic. A child at their hostel was convulsing and needed immediate medical help, they said. I ran to the place which was just a few blocks away. Chinna, a five-year-old, was having typical febrile convulsions, but felt alright after the routine management. That's how I first met this polio stricken boy.

My association with the Government Home for the Crippled began with that visit and it is still going strong. I could never bring myself to break the emotional bond these cheerful kids had built with their doctor. Their innocence, curiosity, warmth of affection, talent in different fields and their indomitable spirit is something that has never ceased to fascinate me. Despite living in the most difficult conditions, away from their homes, these little bundles of joy have given me some of the finest moments of my life.

The boy who had convulsions, Chinna, has two small stumps as his upper limbs. Having lost his mother early in his life, he had learnt how to fend for himself and was exceptionally mature for his age. As he needed to be fed by a caretaker, I often saw him waiting for his turn with a longing look in his eyes. Fed up with this waiting business, he started trying to hold the spoon in between his toes. Soon, holding things like chalk, pencil, coal pieces became his obsession and he mastered the art to perfection.

One day, as I was about to enter the premises, I saw a group of Chinna's friends looking at a paper and laughing away to glory! On my coaxing, they showed me the drawing of a grave looking lady with a stethoscope around her neck. You guessed it right! It was my portrait, replete with minute details of my hairstyle and the typical stern look of a doctor. I was stunned to learn that Chinna had drawn it!

Off I went and bought him a boxful of crayons and paints; and his eyes gleamed with excitement. A discerning drawing teacher staying close by agreed to hone his tremendous talent. Soon, Chinna became a regular at all local and national-level competitions; nobody could believe that the drawings were made with a pencil held with his toes! His Doctor Didi often became the first viewer of his creations.

My joyous pride knew no bounds when he won a National Art Fellowship and joined a famous art school in Delhi. He now holds solo exhibitions at various art galleries across India. The shy, tiny bud has blossomed into a confident young artist, never conscious of how much of an inspiration he has become for many who join the shelter every year. The Government Home for the Crippled now boasts of an acclaimed singer, an athlete, and a rangoli artist. I have long stopped to be just a doctor for them and more a didi.

I have erased the words 'crippled' and 'handicapped' from my dictionary. Chinna and the others have forced me to do so!

Dr Shubhada Sanjay Khirwadkar

Special Bonds

'Aaah!' she yelled as her finger got trapped in a kitchen drawer. It was a nasty cut but nothing could stop Varshaben from reaching the Centre on time today. She soaked some cotton wool in Savlon and swabbed away the growing ruby droplets on her finger. She threw on her dupatta, picked up her bag, rushed down to her scooter and tried to calm down as she waited at the first signal.

As a physiotherapist for special children, she had learnt to stay focused yet aloof from her work. This was vital. It was the easiest thing to succumb to their wails or protests as she coaxed their often-uncontrollable limbs into defined movements. Even after months of regular physical therapy, results could be unpredictable and slow. She needed nerves of steel to counsel the mothers with their heart-breaking stories as they struggled against society and, at times, their own families to get therapy.

Varshaben helped the children crawl, stand up, walk and eat independently — often a physically and emotionally draining experience. The kids called her 'Varshaben', never 'Doctor', and they were always her 'children', never patients!

Abhi's tawny eyes, garbled speech and hugs had broken through the emotional fence Varshaben had erected, as easily as had her own first-born. This explained her anxiety because today was an important day; she had planned to get Abhi to take her first independent steps.

Would Abhi be able to make it past the few metres between the parallel bars? Did she have sufficient control over her spastic muscles? Should she wait for some more time? The time for questions was over — Abhi was waiting for her as she reached the Centre and had saved the last jalebi and fafda for her as usual.

'Abhi wants to walk in her new sequinned shoes, Varshaben. Can she?' Abhi's mother asked.

'Hmmm… Abhi, why don't you walk towards those shoes and then wear them?'

Reluctantly, Abhi agreed and they got her ready to take her first steps in fifteen years. Abhi struggled out of the wheelchair with her splints and boots and her mother placed the glittering pair at the end of the parallel bars.

Abhi had wanted to walk in those shiny shoes for a long time. Determined, she grasped the bars and commanded her unwilling limbs to support her. Varshaben made final adjustments to the straps so they wouldn't cut into Abhi's delicate feet. She stood outside the bars but said nothing.

There was complete silence in the room. No cajoling, no encouragements. Abhi was mesmerised by the beckoning pair of shoes as she set out towards them. The only sound was of Abhi's laboured rapid breathing and the tap of her shoes as she took one excruciating step after another. The sequinned shoes dazzled in the morning sunlight that streamed in through the window.

Abhi was wet with sweat and was muttering under her breath; Varshaben could barely understand Abhi's words over the sound of her thudding heart as she silently counted down the steps …

'Three.'

'Two.'

'Ma…'

Abhi was enveloped in her mother's arms, both crying as if their hearts would explode. Varshaben wiped her eyes as she let Abhi savour the joy of her debut walk.

Abhi sank back into the wheelchair but her face glowed with joy as her mother helped her put on the shiny pair of shoes. Varshaben and her mother admired her now sparkling feet. The spunky mother-daughter duo had overcome much family ridicule to reach this stage.

Varshaben did not regret having let down her emotional guard. It was achievements like this that helped her see the world as special children do, and she thanked god for letting her be a part of their lives. These bonds were special indeed!

Archana Pande

The Magic Potion

Most kids, with the exception of a few brave-hearts, are naturally petrified of barbers and doctors. I was no exception. The scissors and the syringe were my sworn enemies. Being a girl, I could escape the former many times but vaccinations were a loathsome yet unavoidable part of my life. I have no memory of my reactions in the first four years of my life but Mom says my piercing cries each time I was jabbed were enough to shatter the eardrums of those in the vicinity.

We shifted to a different locality the year I turned five. I had to go for my booster shot and that too, to a new doctor. That was the most dreaded part of my young life; I remember clutching Mom's sari and peering from behind her with an ashen face and terrified eyes. And I found myself staring into a pair of the kindest eyes.

I instantly warmed up to Dr Mukherji but that did not lessen my fear a single bit. As he prepared to give me the shot, I prepared to shriek my lungs out. Perhaps anticipating my screams, he quickly said, 'I promise to give you magic syrup if you prove that you are a brave girl.'

The temptation was enough for me to try to control my vocal cords. Amazingly, it did not hurt at all, or perhaps I was too busy thinking about the 'magic' syrup to pay attention to the inoculation. Whatever the reason, the idea worked. I went home, the proud owner of a magic potion. The burgundy colour syrup tasted yummy too. After that I lost my fear of doctors and needles. Soon I became a regular at Dr Mukherji, or rather Dr Uncle's clinic, whether I was unwell or just accompanying some ailing family member.

Every fortnight I would visit him under some pretext or the other to get a refill of the potion, and he would always be happy to oblige. This went on for five years and a strong bond developed between us. Sadly, Dad's job came in the way; we had to shift yet again. I still remember the emotional farewell when I visited his clinic for the last time before moving.

Dabbing his eyes, he said, 'I have three sons but always longed for a daughter. You are the daughter I never had.'

Time flew. I got married, had kids and moved to Chennai. I got busy with my life, yet Kolkata and Dr Mukherji's words always resonated at the back of my mind.

So when I had to fly to Kolkata for a close friend's wedding I got a godsend opportunity to meet my favourite man. I was visiting the clinic after nearly twenty years but everything was the same.

Yet there was a major change. Dr Mukherji no longer sat in the clinic, his son did. Dispelling my awkwardness I told him the purpose of my visit.

'Yes, of course. I know you very well. Baba keeps talking about you even now. Would you like to meet him?'

I could only nod as words failed me completely. The

house was just beyond the clinic. I could hardly contain my excitement as I rang the doorbell. A maid opened it. I was led straight to his study where he was reading a book.

'Welcome, my child,' he said getting up slowly. Age had caught up with him; each one of his eighty years showed on his wrinkled face, stooped stance and wrinkled hands. Yet his eyes were still the same — twinkling with humour and shining with kindness.

We chatted for two hours. Well, I did most of the chatting and he listened with an indulgent smile. There was so much to tell him. At last, it was time to leave. As I got up he said, 'Here is your potion. This time it is for your daughter, to help her to become brave like her mother and face the world proudly.'

Smiling through my tears, I asked him, 'What are the ingredients of this miracle drink?'

'Three parts grape juice and one part love,' he replied, eyes twinkling.

Smita Shenoy

The Silent Thief

Being an ophthalmologist, people come to me with the hope that their vision will be restored so that they can lead better lives. Some of the patients are at a stage where their sight has been reduced to the minimal, but still their expectations are high. 'You are God for us. God had given me eyes to see and I have lost them; you will be the second God in our lives,' they say.

I was writing a thesis on glaucoma, a disease which is very deceptive as you don't realise the damage it can do until the vision starts becoming weak. It is actually 'the silent thief'. Soren Singh was my first critical case of this syndrome. He was sixty-three years old, tall, and held a wooden stick in his hand. He always wore suspenders, which made him look younger. Despite having lost most of his vision, Soren Singh was a jovial and easy-going old chap. He would laugh off things and make even difficult situations seem so simple. During the course of our interactions, I started looking up to him.

Sorenji's eyesight was almost gone; I had tried everything I could, but all I could manage was to prolong his partial vision for a few more months. Soon he would turn completely blind, it was inevitable.

'Your name is Jyoti, and just as your name suggests, you bring light in the life of others,' were his recurring words to me. Sorenji came on the first Saturday of every month. We bonded over black tea and soon he became more like a father figure to me. He would often talk about his only son who was in America.

During one session, Sorenji told me, 'Dr Jyoti, before I turn blind, I want to go and see the Taj Mahal in Agra.'

'Sorenji you will surely see it, don't worry,' I spoke reassuringly, but deep inside I knew that if his wish was not fulfilled immediately, it would remain only a dream.

I called his son in America who disappointed me when he said, 'Doctor, I am sorry I can't come all the way to India to take my father to see the Taj Mahal!'

But I was determined to make it happen. If not his son, I would take him. It was a thought, which had never occurred to me for any of my other patients. I spoke to my husband about it.

'My parents died when I was three. Our religion tells us that if you fulfil your parents' desires, their blessings stay with you for a life time. Sorenji is like my father. He wants to see the Taj Mahal and I would like to take him before he loses his eyesight.' Vivek agreed immediately and even offered to come along with us. So the three of us went to see the Taj Mahal.

Sorenji was delighted and his eyes welled with tears. He became blind after a few months of his visit to the Taj Mahal.

Sometimes this profession can be humbling; despite having the power to save or improve lives, there are times when we are helpless. That is the time we realise that our competence is trivial in front of His and we have no choice but to bow down to Him.

For me, Sorenji was just not a subject of study; he had become a part of my family. He lives in my thoughts and every time I discover 'the silent thief' in my patients, my heart leaps and I go to all lengths to save their eyesight.

As told to Arti Sonthalia

The Extra Mile

My good friend Sia's parents' acrimonious divorce had brought her closer to her mother than ever before. Her mother enveloped her teenage daughter in love and security. Supermom, she was called, and she certainly lived up to that moniker. Trying to be both mom and dad, she worked round the clock. Her day started at 6 a.m., getting work done around the house before she dropped Sia to college and left for her office. Back home at 5 p.m. she would get busy trying out yummy recipes for her daughter, going through the bills and planning small investments for their future. At dinner, she would be all ears as Sia narrated the happenings of the day.

One morning she could not get up. Her back ached unbearably and she had slight fever. 'Mom, you look pale and exhausted. You stay in bed and I'll take care of everything. All you need is rest.' Sia was a bit nervous but she put up a brave front.

Days turned into weeks. Painkillers gave temporary relief to the backache but the fever persisted. They visited the doctor who suggested blood tests and a CT scan. The blood reports showed an alarmingly low level of haemoglobin and the CT scan revealed glands in her rib cage. A series of tests were run before the doctor gravely announced the glands as malignant.

Sia's head throbbed and stomach churned as she picked up her phone and called her father. They needed him here with them. After talking to her dad, Sia hung up with trembling hands. He was in America on work and couldn't come back before a fortnight. He hadn't sounded too disturbed either. She collapsed into a chair and cried with her face hidden in her palms; she couldn't handle this on her own.

Sia felt a hand on her head. She looked up to see Dr Gandhi, the oncologist. He asked her to meet him in his office in fifteen minutes. There was something comforting about his persona. He was a short, fair-skinned, fifty-something man with silver hair and a face that exuded compassion. He spoke to Sia at length about the outcome of this disease and explained that medical science had advanced by leaps and bounds, making it possible for even cancer patients to live a quality life. By God's grace, her mother's cancer had been detected at an early stage, which meant that with chemotherapy, a strict diet and medication, she could be free of the disease.

Sia felt a trickle of relief, but she had a thousand questions. She hesitated as the doctor was obviously a busy man, but he asked her to go on. After answering her questions patiently, he made a call. Within a few minutes, a middle-aged woman walked into his office. 'Sia, this is Anjali and I want you to spend some time with her before we talk again.' Anjali shook hands with Sia and led her out of the doctor's office.

Sia followed Anjali mechanically until she realised that they were at the hospital café. 'Let's grab a bite before we meet some people,' Anjali said as she ordered sandwiches and cold coffee. She was an amiable and vivacious woman who spoke about how it was possible to live life on one's own terms. And then Sia learned that Anjali, at thirty five, was a blood cancer survivor. Anjali had obviously been shattered when she was told about her disease; she had her entire life yet to be lived. But she had battled her disease with grit and positivity, and survived. And now, at the behest of Dr Gandhi, she served as a part-time counsellor at the hospital for patients as well as their relatives.

Sia hadn't realised how hungry she was until she started to eat the food on her plate. Then they took the elevator to the day care in the basement. Anjali introduced Sia to two patients who were survivors of the same disease, and their relatives. It was an enlightening experience as Sia learnt that there was hope, and a lot depended on the kind of affirmative support she would lend her mother. After spending three hours with Anjali, she felt composed. Thanking her profusely, Sia went up to be with her mother.

The next day I visited Sia's mother at the hospital. To my surprise, Sia was no longer the mental wreck she had been when I had last met her two days back. She told me all about her positive interaction with Anjali and we went down to Dr Gandhi's office to thank him.

'Dr Gandhi, I feel I can now help my mom fight this and I have a good feeling that she will make it,' she expressed her gratitude.

'I'm just doing my job. Day in and day out, I break the worst news possible to people. They cry, go into shock and sometimes loathe me for it. Anjali is my bond with my patients. While I work on their body, she nurses their mind, which plays a very important role in their healing process,' he replied with a smile.

Dr Gandhi may believe that he was just doing his job, but through Anjali he had given my friend conviction and a new perspective of life. Where her dad had failed her, Dr Gandhi, an outsider, had gone that extra mile to strengthen her.

Swati Rajgharia

3

BRINGING NEW LIVES INTO THE WORLD

A baby is God's opinion that the world should go on.

—Carl Sandburg

A Mentor in Need

'Life changes post pregnancy' is an understatement. Apart from the mammoth transformation that a mom-to-be's body goes through, she also has to contend with changing relationship equations as the tiny tot takes over her life completely. And it doesn't get better the second time around, as I found out first-hand. I was just picking up my life from where I had left off after I'd had my first child, when the stork decided to visit again.

The moment the home test kit showed two red bands, the world as I knew it went on a long holiday. As morning sickness, bloating and cravings struck my body with vengeance, I was totally lost. The hormonal fluctuations made me emotionally vulnerable, and the fact that my girlfriends were busy with their lives and careers made me feel more alienated with each passing day.

And then the barrage of advice started pouring in from all quarters; even distant relations put in their sixpence worth: drink saffron-laced milk to ensure the baby has soft skin, eat a gooseberry a day for thick locks, have fresh cream to guarantee a creamy complexion, and so on. My head spun and my body protested from trying to follow all these instructions, and this crazy pattern continued for two months till I decided to consult a gynaecologist.

When I met Dr Shobana, I understood why she was one of the leading obstetricians in Chennai. Calm, collected and dignified, she exuded confidence. She immediately put me at ease and handled all my questions, doubts and complaints patiently.

During my second visit to her clinic, I was going through a bout of pre-natal blues. I asked her, 'Why does the second pregnancy feel so difficult? Considering I already have a child, the second time around should be a breeze, right?'

'All of us feel that experience makes us better equipped to handle the subsequent pregnancy but that is not strictly true. Some facets will definitely be common but each pregnancy is as different as chalk and cheese. I will be there to guide you at every step, so don't worry.

'No matter what people tell you, just follow my advice and you will be fine,' she said with a knowing smile. And I did just that.

Under her tutelage I sailed through the remaining seven months. She helped me come to terms with my changing body, she made me sign up for pre-natal classes where I bonded with other would-be-moms and forged some friendships for life. A supervised diet took care of the nausea, heartburns and discomfiture.

Despite her hectic schedule, she always answered my panic calls and replied to those crazy, midnight SOS messages. Of course, in hindsight I realised that some of the SMSs had been quite inane, but when you are pregnant everything seems like an emergency!

On the 6th of December when I held my bonny baby in my arms, I knew I had only one person to thank — the lady in white, my doctor and mentor.

Smita Shenoy

Birth on the Berth of a Train

We were all sitting in the suburban train bound for CST Mumbai. The best part of travelling in a train in Mumbai is the company; strong friendships and bonds form because you spend most of your travel time with these people. The train was on time and I had got in at Mulund, a Mumbai suburb. I was the last one to get into the train and the group was complete. As usual someone had got home-made food and was passing it around. Two of us fancied ourselves as singers and were straining our voices over the usual commotion.

Suddenly, from behind us, we heard a woman's scream and all of us craned our necks to see what had happened. What we saw was unbelievable! There was a pregnant lady probably near her due date: her water bag had burst and she was in labour! It was a fast train and yet the next station was almost twenty minutes away. There was an immediate scurry of ladies asking if anyone was a doctor.

I was in the final year of MBBS and hence the chosen one to help the woman, Shiela. This was a real case which I needed to handle; I took a deep breath and told my friend,

Priya, to first clear everybody from around Shiela. Secondly I asked for clothes that could be used as a makeshift curtain around the lady. Most of the ladies gave their stoles and we covered Shiela somewhat. The next task was to sanitise my hands and check out the basic instruments required; luckily I had carried my medical box which had most of the things that I would need.

Shiela was in excruciating pain. We needed to keep her relaxed so that her blood pressure wouldn't shoot up. I shooed the rest of the ladies away and only Priya, another elderly lady and I were around to help in the delivery.

Looking at Shiela, I said, 'Don't worry, we are all in this together. We need your support and everything will be all right.' Sheila managed to smile through her pain. After adjusting her properly I could see the crown of the baby. 'Keep pushing, Sheila, I can see the crown of the baby's head,' I encouraged her while Priya dabbed cold water on her face and neck. Seeing that it was taking time, many women suggested that we pull the chain to stop the train, but I ignored them. My whole concentration was on the baby.

My hands were trembling; the elderly lady, Sarla Ben, was encouraging me and Sheila saying that God was with us. Priya was dabbing Sheila's forehead with cologne water and Sarla Ben was pushing at the apex of her stomach to help the baby out. Finally after much effort, the baby was born.

Just holding the baby in my arms was so miraculous, I started weeping. The wailing of the child brought me back to reality and blinking away my tears, I cut the umbilical cord. The baby was a robust boy with a thatch of black hair. With the first wail of the baby boy, the whole compartment cheered and started clapping loudly, and that's when I realised that the compartment had been silent for so long.

The slowing down of the train indicated the coming of the next station. Unbelievably, the delivery had taken exactly twenty minutes.

I was in a daze when we reached the station. Some of the other ladies helped Sheila to get down from the train and took her to the nearby hospital. All the remaining ladies patted our backs and gave us glasses of water. Priya looked at me and said, 'Kaya, we did it!'

I was crying and smiling at the same time. Till date I remember that delivery on a train berth. Later Sheila called to thank me, and I met her family at her home. They named the boy Veer and Indian Railways passed a resolution to gift him a lifetime of free travel anywhere in India.

Now I am an established gynaecologist settled in London and have been delivering babies for a long time, but Veer will always remain my most memorable baby.

As told to Jyoti Kerkar

Docs Don't Cry

Under the Hippocratic Oath, a doctor pledges to ensure ethical conduct. One of the outcomes of this oath happens to be emotional detachment towards patients.

When I came to Hyderabad with my wife Sutapa, we started looking for a good gynaecologist, since we were planning a second child. Two of my office colleagues praised one Dr S and her extraordinary abilities, and so we decided to visit her.

Dr S's chamber was full of patients and I wondered if she was good enough to justify the consultancy fee, which was rather expensive. When our turn came, we found that Dr S, who appeared to be in her fifties, was a simple, unassuming, bespectacled lady. She spoke encouragingly to us and suggested a few vitamins for my wife.

A few months later, Sutapa conceived, but during the second month of the pregnancy, she was diagnosed with low-lying placenta, and consequently Dr S advised her to rest as much as possible. Sutapa was eager to go to parents' place in Vadodara, and on every visit, we would ask Dr S: 'Can she go home now? Is the placenta condition any better?'

During the fourth month, Dr S said that the placenta had moved up a bit but we should still avoid travelling. We pleaded that Sutapa would get good care at her parents' place and there would be enough support to ensure her complete rest. After some persuasion, the doctor consented.

Within a few days of reaching Vadodara, Sutapa developed a condition known as complete placenta previa. Her placenta ruptured and she had to be hospitalised; the baby had to be aborted. Sutapa was very weak, having lost a lot of blood. I rushed to Vadodara and brought her back, but the damage was done — she was broken, both mentally and physically.

There would be days when we would just hold each other and cry; we tried to console ourselves and come to terms with our grief by playing with our son but all three of us were heartbroken.

We didn't visit Dr S anymore; we didn't have a reason to.

But then one day, after two months, we did visit her. She heard the whole story, sent me out of the room under the pretext of examining Sutapa and then she just held my wife and wept. Yes, the renowned gynaecologist, bound to the sacred Hippocratic Oath, wept. Later, she called me in and said: 'This is a challenge — I don't want you to give up hope. Try again, and I will be there by your side.'

Months passed. Sutapa conceived again. We started our regular visits to Dr S; she took great care and began prescribing vitamins and medicines to sustain the pregnancy. Again as luck would have it, her placenta was low and Dr S advised bed rest for Sutapa. I took over the household chores to ensure that she strictly followed the doctor's advice.

Once Sutapa entered the second trimester, Dr S announced

that the placenta had moved up but still advised caution; this time we were careful to heed her words.

In the beginning of the ninth month, Sutapa went into labour. Dr S did a quick ultrasound and announced that she needed a caesarean immediately.

After a few hours, while Sutapa was in deep slumber with the new-born baby in a cot next to her, Dr S came into our room and said, 'Now I am happy, I can go to the US. You know my daughter is also expecting but I was worried about Sutapa and did not want to leave her in the care of other doctors. You see, I am going there as a mother, not as a doctor! I will leave you my email address so if you have any post-pregnancy issues, please contact me.'

I wished her well and bade her goodbye, thankful to God for not only giving us a great doctor, but more importantly, a wonderful human being.

Who said that doctors don't cry?

Sutirtha Saha

Lateral Thinking

Before Independence, there was an eminent surgeon, Dr S. Rangachari, in erstwhile Madras Presidency. He was very dedicated and served the public tirelessly. He was a down-to-earth person and would often donate his personal money to poor patients to buy medicines and food. He never bothered about the status or wealth of a patient. He treated the rich and poor alike. His clinic was the most sought-after destination for people with diverse chronic health problems.

Dr Rangachari did not believe in the theory of prescribing lots of medicines just because a patient had come to consult a doctor. He used to cure many diseases and tackle rare medical cases by application of human psychology. With his extensive experience, he had evolved ingenious ways of dealing with his patients.

Once he had to handle a very complicated delivery case. A pregnant woman with labour pains was taken into the operation theatre to be readied for a caesarean delivery. But there was a problem; one of the tiny fingers of the unborn baby was jutting out of the mother's navel. The team of doctors and nurses assisting Dr Rangachari, stood around the pregnant woman deliberating as to how to get the baby out. They were at their wits' end. All of them knew that unless the baby withdrew its finger, safe delivery either naturally or through a cesarean section, was ruled out.

Dr Rangachari was briefed about the problem. He glanced at the site where the baby's tiny finger was jutting out and the anxious look of the mother to-be. This was a rare case in medical history.

He nonchalantly went out of the operation theatre and took the stairs down to the ground floor. He went to a corner and lit a cigarette. He had a puff and brooded about the delivery. How could he make the baby withdraw its finger? Like a flash, an idea occurred to him. He walked back to the operation theatre. He tapped the ash off the cigarette into an empty bowl and very gently moved the cigarette closer to the navel of the pregnant woman and grazed the burning end of the cigarette over the tip of the jutting finger of the baby just for a fraction of a second. And lo — a miracle happened, the unborn baby withdrew its finger! The interns, nurses and doctors who were watching were astounded! They spontaneously started applauding.

Lateral thinking works. In seeking a solution to the problem, everyone in the operation theatre was thinking about the conventional methods in medical science. But Dr Rangachari, though a firm believer in medical science, thought outside the box, and came up with a brilliant solution.

T.S. Karthik

Touched By an Angel

Silent tears streamed down my face and wet the stark white hospital pillow case as the harsh lights of the operation theatre fell on me. They were being rather impolite, I felt. But at that moment the entire world seemed unpleasant. I was scared of the pain. I was terrified of the anaesthesia jab that would be thrust into my spine. It was then that my doctor entered the operation theatre.

He saw my tears and laughed. 'Don't be scared, big girl. People are scared of the unknown, of darkness, and I assure you there will be bright light all around, the light of science and of course, these bulbs ...'

I tried remembering the doctor's words; the seeds of bravery he had tried to sow in me by making everything seem very factual, scientific and regular. But since it was happening to me, it all seemed an aberration! As the needle began to pierce my skin, I tried remembering what he had said but his words disappeared halfway ...

Pregnancy is not a disease, it's very normal...

It is natural, it is definitely not something you need to be scared of...

Ninety per cent of pregnant women experience backaches…

In most medical journals, a modern caesarean operation is almost painless …

The doctor had spoken so much about facts and figures and science; he had also shown me videos and charts. Objectively it had all made sense in his chambers, where chilled orange juice was served in the waiting room. In fact, he had made more sense than my grandmothers, who viewed the entire thing as a blessing and wanted me to pay homage to the family deity every Saturday. But swinging between being an atheist and a conditioned believer, I was totally confused.

Thankfully my sudden bouts of nausea had saved me from pondering about this confusion for the doctor had advised me to think about positive things whenever I was down.

'I always advise my patients to keep away from negative thoughts. Be positive. Don't worry, you will be elated when the baby is born,' he had said through his shell-rimmed glasses while handing me an Anne Geddes post card of little babies dressed in sunflower costumes.

I had smiled, not knowing what else to do. In reality, I was scared. It bothered me that even though I was about to become a mother in a matter of months, I did not feel the right emotions. I did not feel like a mother. Would I be able to care for the baby as my mother had taken care of me? Is there any guarantee that I would love my baby? As my tummy started becoming bigger, more such thoughts began clouding my mind. I tried meditation to get away from such negative thoughts and it seemed to work. But that day while I was in the operation theatre waiting for my baby to be born, it failed.

All the apprehensions that had been growing in me for the past nine months seemed to have returned.

I remembered that a sea of smiling faces had wished me luck as I was taken inside the OT on a stretcher. I had smiled though all I wanted to do was wail like a baby and well, maybe run away. Absolutely helpless, I closed my eyes and instinctively prayed, oblivious to everything that was happening to me. As I prayed every few minutes, it dawned upon me that it was a long time since I had last done this. That ever since college, I had stopped believing ... even though my mind was conditioned otherwise. This was exactly when I felt a tug below my chest, where the baby's feet supposedly were ...

Is the anaesthesia wearing off?

Are they taking my kidneys out?

Or is it my lungs?

Oh God, the doctor's messed up!

Seconds later, I heard a wail, which was more cat-like than human. The cry simply stunned me and I forgot all my apprehensions, the pain and the general discomfort. It had seemed hours (though everybody later claimed it was just a few minutes) till the doctor came forward. He held in his hand a small crying baby whose nose flared up in the same manner as my husband's. I remained frozen though my eyes kept moving to observe the baby, to record in my memory every minute detail I had seen.

'It's a boy!'

After that I became drowsy and things were a bit hazy. It seemed as if the lights were becoming brighter and a hundred suns and moons and stars were shining to receive my baby. Even the doctor in his white hospital gown was fading away.

For a moment he seemed to be an angel who had brought the baby to me from God himself.

Even now, I can't describe how I felt when I saw my baby — all I could think then was that it can't be science that created the baby. It must have been a miracle; God's miracle delivered my baby through his angel, the doctor. I decided I would tell him this but before he came back I was fast asleep.

'Thank you for protecting me throughout my pregnancy and delivering my son,' I told the doctor when he came to visit me later. Under my breath I muttered, 'Like an angel'.

He said, 'It was my duty. Any other doctor in my place would have done the same.'

When he was gone I lay thinking, with my son by my side. After my baby's arrival, I needed time off from everybody and the hospital confinement allowed me just that. It was during this time I realised something: it isn't easy to become a doctor and everybody doesn't get the opportunity. Like God had chosen my son to be my son, he has chosen some people to be doctors. It could be true that since it wasn't possible for God to send white-winged haloed angels to help us, he gave us doctors.

Suddenly I was happy. Not in an ecstatic way but in a more calm manner. A miracle had indeed happened and yes, I had been touched by an angel. Thank you again, dear doctor.

Joie Bose Chatterjee

4

GREAT EXPECTATIONS

Medicine is the only profession that labours incessantly to destroy the reason for its own existence.

–James Bryce

A Piece of Bread

I hail from a humble background and those were days of adversity. My father was an honest man with a lot of integrity, who was struggling to make ends meet. I was at the impressionable age of twelve when my uncle visited us. He got me an issue of the *Reader's Digest* magazine, which was an indulgence for someone like me, as we could barely afford our daily meals. It was quite a treat and I savoured every page of that magazine, little knowing that one of the stories would determine my future.

It was a story by Dr Christian Bernard, the renowned cardiac surgeon. It was the year 1976 and cardiac surgery was just evolving at that time. Dr Bernard was scheduled to perform a heart surgery on a nine-year-old boy, which took him into a reflective disposition.

'There is a malfunctioning valve in the boy's heart which I will fix and that will give him life. I will be God as I give him a new lease of life.' With such egocentric thoughts, he walked into the operation theatre. The little boy had not been given any

food (as is the norm before most surgeries)
to the doctor that he was hungry.

82

'I want a piece of bread,' he said. Dr B
him that once the surgery was over, he cou
wanted to, but right now he could not giv   ...y ...ng. Dr
Bernard confidently set out to do the surgery, but during the
course of it, the boy died.

Dr Bernard was wallowing in a state of skepticism when he
thought to himself, 'We talk about doing great things but are
we really that great, and can we ever be God? I was planning
to give life to this little child but I could not even give him a
piece of bread.'

This story had a profound impact on me. I began to marvel at
this profession and since that day I started reading everything
I could on cardiac surgery. And each book I read after this story
made me sure of one thing — deep down in my heart I know
what I want to be, a cardiac surgeon.

Dr Anil Jain

Anywhere at All

We were in a rattling, overcrowded bus winding our way across the Ghats. A couple of the villagers were sick and throwing up out of the windows with abandon. The smell choked us. At the next stop, my classmate, Girish, got some anti-nausea medicines out of his haversack and offered them to all those who were feeling queasy, so that we could have some comfort for the next couple of hours.

When the bus started its journey again, a middle-aged man with pockmarks all over his cheeks, and wearing a city-tailored shirt and pant, asked him what he did for a living.

'Doctor,' came my classmate's reply. From then on, Girish had to field questions about dyspepsia, foot drop, infertility, wax coming out of the ears, falling hair, backaches ... problems not just about the man himself, but about his brothers, his sister's children, wife's family and all other relatives that came to his mind.

When he ran out of relatives, he graciously permitted another passenger to take his seat and place so he could make full use of the dear 'Daakter' whilst the bus continued towards its destination. Everybody took their turn. By the end of the journey, without any examination, and without even being present, several 'patients', mostly by proxy, had been diagnosed and the prognosis cheerfully given.

One or two were declared 'back from Yama' and everyone in the bus was happy at the thought. At the end of the ride, a grateful segment of rural India's population offered the good doctor a hen, some potatoes, a bagful of peanuts, firewood, and a used but warm scarf.

'Where do you practice?' I had once asked my doctor friend.

'Anywhere at all,' had been the prompt reply. The moment someone finds out that a person is a doctor, symptoms come tumbling out, from headaches that have not been cured for years, heartaches that have lingered for months, near-death experiences, to even boils in unmentionable areas. Add to that opinions on ancient traditional methods of treatment versus toxic capsules that one consumes these days and you have a veritable university set up in someone's dining room at a late-night party.

What's more, a doctor's a doctor no matter what is his or her specialisation. At dinners and parties, paediatricians are asked questions about skin problems, dermatologists are asked to give their opinions on heart ailments. Nothing like a free consultation! I guess gynaecologists are the only ones spared. Somehow 'friendly' advice seems more genuine than a 'professional' consultation.

It isn't easy for any human being to live up to such expectations. No wonder then, they live in their cocooned worlds, not easily mingling with self-confessed lesser mortals. For if they didn't, they would be constantly at work — answering questions about health issues, real or imagined, with no boundaries of time or location — anytime, anywhere.

Sheela Jaywant

Doctor of Hearts

It is 10 p.m. and the buzzer bell goes tring, tring, tring — three times — indicating an emergency, when the doctor and his family are having dinner. Suddenly, there is commotion and action in Dr Kagal's upstairs flat.

Leaving his dinner half-finished, rushing barefoot down the stairs, he runs to the ward from where the emergency signal had come. There on the cot is a man surrounded by nervous nurses, who immediately move aside when the doctor reaches the spot.

The patient, who has had a cardiac arrest and could be gone in a few seconds, is given a rigorous massage and pumping on the chest by Dr Kagal. Then electric shock is applied; the atmosphere is tense and pin-drop silence prevails in the room.

The suspense is unbearable for me; I too ran behind Dr Kagal and am watching the drama with bated breath. It's the first time in my life that I have witnessed such a scenario. Slowly, the man breathes a sigh, opens his eyes and looks around. His breathing is now more regular and Dr Kagal straightens from his bent posture and greets the patient cheerily, 'Namaskaar

Patil saheb, how are you?' A faint smile radiates from that drained face and acknowledges the greeting, so to say.

My husband and I often went to Belgaum, a beautiful city in Karnataka, since my husband's eldest brother and his wife had settled there with their son, Dr Anil Kagal, who had started Kagal Hospital from their ground floor residence. An MD gold medalist from Mumbai, this heart specialist had opted to settle in a remote small city in Karnataka, despite getting job offers from the posh hospitals of Mumbai.

I had heard about cardiac arrest stories from Anil, when the heart actually stops beating and the person is almost dead, but how just a crucial few seconds of immediate therapy can mean a matter of life and death.

Mr Patil, overjoyed at being given a second lease of life, promised his saviour an acre of land from his huge property, just a few minutes after the tense drama of life and death had ended. His recovery was fast and he went home in about ten days. But after a year, he was back with another heart attack and once again the cardiac arrest crisis took place, I was told. And another promise of one more acre of land!

We teased Anil, saying he was indeed a rich man after owning so much land. The doctor had a big laugh and said, 'Do you think I take him seriously? Neither does Mr Patil himself. It's a dying man's promise and he forgets it when he gets well, and so do I. It is all part of our profession!'

Kunda Kagal

Doctored

I was a nine-year-old living in Bangalore. My father wasn't keeping too well and I think that was the reason I would constantly wish I had an older brother who was a doctor. My younger brother seemed most unlikely to turn into a pillar of the Indian professional society, more commonly known as a doctor.

I was surrounded by boys in our locality and my friend and I felt extremely outnumbered. The mothers of the boys always looked strangely at us, the awkward looking girls, especially one Mrs Khan who looked like a porcelain doll.

Once I bumped into her at the market and while making polite conversation, she asked me, 'What do you plan to do when you grow up?' Instantly I said, 'Become a doctor' and her eyes grew wide in surprise with a hint of admiration.

'Your parents must be relieved and happy,' she continued. Complaints of my younger brother's playful ways had obviously reached her ears.

I decided I needed to really impress Mrs Khan, so I made up an older brother on the spot who was a doctor studying at Stanley Medical College in Chennai. One of our distant relatives was the personality on whom I modelled this so-called 'brother'. I knew I had really scored brownie points with the beautiful Mrs Khan, who invited me to her house the next day and gave me orange squash and sugar biscuits which I loved. My 'older brother' seemed to have done the trick.

I waxed eloquent about how he would take care of my dad and his path-breaking medical research. Mrs Khan looked impressed enough to marry her daughter off to him (if she had one, of course). For a month I feasted regularly on orange squash and sugar biscuits and hobnobbed with the porcelain beauty. It went on beautifully till my mother decided to accept Mrs Khan's invitation for tea.

Before I knew it, my mother was home, furious and disappointed that her daughter was turning out to be a pathological liar. Needless to say, I suffered Mrs Khan's shocked silent treatment. Sadly, the goodies also stopped.

I went back to my mundane world. I was grounded by my parents for a month after that, and lectured about the importance of speaking the truth.

Of course after that incident I stopped fibbing, but I still retain this figment of my imagination — my 'elder brother' who is a doctor on a mission to save the world. He became my hope for a better tomorrow and an inspiration to achieve something in life. You may call it a delusion, but not all role models are made up of flesh and blood. Some can be conjured and it might just be what the doctor ordered.

Madhuri Jagadeesh

Magical Hands

'It's a baby boy,' Mehar told the waiting relatives of the woman she had just operated on, and in an instant their faces turned jubilant.

'You have magical hands, Doctor,' one of the women spoke from behind her burkha. Mehar smiled and walked towards her cabin. Her thoughts turned to Varun, her only son, and she wondered why her 'magic' had not worked with him. She had been apprehensive about him since she had returned from London, but try as she might, he refused to reveal what it was that was upsetting him.

Raghav, Mehar's husband, had been very supportive and had agreed to take care of Varun while she pursued further studies in London. Raghav had always wanted Varun to become a doctor like Mehar and him, so he was determined to start training his son for the future.

Raghav started waking Varun up at four in the morning to study. He insisted that Varun immediately get down to work once he was back from school and Varun was not allowed to play his favourite sports. He had been the captain of his cricket team, but Varun had to leave everything in order to study the way his father wanted him to. If Varun's friends called to speak to him, Raghav told them, 'Varun is studying, don't distract him by calling.'

Varun soon became aloof and detached. His friends were not allowed to meet him except during school hours. He started feeling claustrophobic. Raghav's constant reminder — 'Varun, I want you to be a doctor and you have to work very hard' — upset him to no end. His heart ached for his mother; he missed the after-dinner talks with Mehar in which he could say anything that was on his mind. He knew he could talk to her on the phone, but he didn't want to bother her when she was already so worked up about her studies.

Mehar returned and was shocked to see a new Varun. He hardly spoke more than a few syllables. He didn't join Mehar and Raghav for meals, instead preferring to eat alone. The jovial, full of life, ever-excited Varun had become reserved, un-communicative and lonely.

Mehar spoke to Raghav, but all he said was, 'I think it is because he didn't get the desired marks even after studying so hard.'

Mehar knew it was more than that. She spoke with Dr Reema, a psychiatrist, who told her to not force him in any way. 'He needs friends,' she had said. 'Why don't you ask him whether he really wants to become a doctor?'

Mehar realised Varun had never told her that he had wanted to be a doctor. Cricket had always been his priority. Perhaps her son wanted to be a cricketer. Mehar understood that this was where the problem lay. Raghav had been under the assumption that, since he and Mehar were doctors, Varun would *have* to become a doctor.

That evening, while going back home, Mehar bought a new cricket bat for Varun. He was thrilled to see it, but he asked Mehar, 'Mom who would I play with? Dad doesn't allow my friends to come over to play.'

'Don't worry Varun, call up all your friends and arrange for a match tomorrow morning, and I shall lay out breakfast for all of you.'

Varun was ecstatic about the whole idea. He had not been so exhilarated in a long time.

Slowly Mehar stopped Raghav from compelling Varun to study. Raghav was furious when she told him about Dr Reema's views, but Mehar knew she wanted her son back — and was willing to fight with Raghav for it.

Varun's eyes regained their gleam. He started talking to Mehar. They became close again and Varun finally revealed his fears and how he had never wanted to become a doctor. Raghav's pressure had bothered him so much, he said, that his mind had been in a state of chaos.

Varun got better marks, he played cricket more often, had a bunch of friends and was like any other boy of his age. Varun eventually became a pilot and now soars high in the sky. He was finally able to do what he truly wanted.

Mehar's magic had finally worked.

Arti Sonthalia

The Letters

'I had the dream again — you were in a yellow sari with a white coat and a pink rose in your hair.'

Malli would receive a letter every week, in her mother's flowery hand, with the 'filmy' vision being the inevitable postscript in each and every letter.

The letters to Malli were weekly snapshots of life in the village, filled with her mother's take on everyone in their huge family and her mother's dreams. Before becoming the daughter-in-law of a zamindar, her mother, Kala, had been a fifteen-year-old filled with dreams of a career which could never take off because of her marriage. In due course, the mantle had been passed on to her daughter.

Malli had been sent away at an early age to the best school in the city. Her ultimate destination, of course, was medical college. Kala routinely poured out her hopes and dreams into the letters, which were to become the sole factor in defining her daughter's life. But when she reached pre-university, Malli started dreading them — for the first time in her life, she began to feel the weight of her mother's dreams.

She *had* to become a doctor. Her own secret wish of studying English Literature seemed too tame a dream to even mention to her mother, who'd dreamt of the white coat and pink rose for ever so long now.

So Malli went on to medical college. She was from a reputed school and had her parents' wealth to support her. But none of these seemed to make any difference in this new world.

Back in school she had a small selective group of friends, and was a favourite among the teachers. But in medical school, she was one among many students, and all the others seemed more intelligent. Her 'convent' English and stately manners did not cut any ice here. All that was needed was hard work, brains and more hard work. Some students were children of doctors with generations of medical background while a few others were students from small schools, who'd come through by dint of sheer hard work.

Malli was somewhere in between; she neither had doctor parents nor the brilliance. She just had the letters, filled with her mother's dreams. She'd imbibed them for so long now that she could hardly distinguish her mother's fantasies from her own.

The subjects were vast, and there was a lot to learn, so Malli began studying each day to cover all the subjects as best as she could. She worked feverishly just to keep up.

Slowly her efforts began to pay off. She rarely moved to the top of her class, but she was never at the bottom either. The prayer that was on her lips for the next five years was — 'let me be part of the regular group'. Failing a year was unimaginable. By the end of her third year, Malli was firmly entrenched in the 'above average' grade of her class, and Kala would brag shamelessly to all and sundry about her soon-to-be-doctor daughter. She clearly didn't realise just what her daughter was going through to make her mother's dream come true.

With the end of the third year, came marriage proposals. The letters were full of platitudes on the alliance — 'You need a husband who's a doctor, and we've found just the right person. We really shouldn't wait; we'll help you out, life is much easier if you have a supportive husband.' A distracted Malli agreed. After many years had passed by, she often wondered why. Perhaps it was a deeply ingrained habit of being subservient to the persuasive letters. Or maybe it was also her prospective husband's good-natured charm or just fate.

Contrary to her expectations, marriage didn't prove to be as distracting as she'd feared. There were snide comments from some of her professors, but her mother had been right on one count at least — it was a relief to have someone who understood the difficulties of studying medicine. The fourth year passed in marital bliss amid the grind of text books.

The letters now resounded with requests for a grandchild. Malli ignored them as long as she could but their tug, combined with her own yearning for a baby, proved too much for her. Against her better judgment, Malli arrived at the dreaded fifth year with a baby on its way and her system awash with hormones.

To her embarrassment, she fainted at the sight of blood one day, and had to be carried out by her classmates. She cried every day, because of the workload, but mostly without any reason at all. Due to a cruel quirk of fate, her obstetrics specialty coincided with her eighth month of pregnancy, and she had to stand for hours watching women in labour scream their way to motherhood, until a sympathetic teacher waived her practical hours. But the impression was vivid. Her own delivery didn't seem as difficult and compared to the advent of her finals, the baby's arrival was a breeze. Malli was soon the mother of a scrawny daughter.

With the delivery out of her way, Malli found herself facing the final exams that were just a month away. A hysterical Malli combated postpartum blues and pre-exam jitters in the only way she knew how — studying feverishly, making timetables she rarely could keep up with because of the incessant demands of a newborn, and falling back on her old prayer — 'please let me graduate with the regular group.'

There is probably some supernatural power that caters to the prayers of first-time mothers in the final year of medical school. Malli's preparation for this year had not been as thorough ... she had studied very selectively but found to her amazement that she could actually answer all the questions.

The last exam was viva voce, conducted by a group of professors at their menacing best. Malli hung around the corridors, watching as one classmate after another came out ashen-faced after their ordeal.

Soon it was Malli's turn. She went in and took her place across her pharmacology professor — a grumpy old doctor well known for his discipline. An average performer, Malli had remained virtually unknown until marriage hauled her into cruel limelight, and made her a target for the professor's famed bluntness — he'd told her she'd end up a 'housewife'. Her fears combined with her progressing pregnancy had kept her away from him, until now.

'So madam,' he boomed, 'how is your baby?' Malli stuttered her reply.

'Before starting your examination, I'd like to say something,' he paused, and looked around at his nodding colleagues. 'I just want to say just how much we all admire your grit. Medical college by itself is difficult, but to face it along with marriage and a child is phenomenal. In fact, I was almost sure you'd quit … but you didn't. Yes, I still think you could have held off your marriage and motherhood, but well, you did it, my dear … well done.'

Malli was almost numb with relief. All those years of doubt and hard work, and it came down to this. She got through those exams, of course. My mother always did get through sticky situations. She still does. At twenty-one, Malli was a doctor, wife and mother of a little girl — me.

And it was finally her turn to write a letter of dreams now — telling my grandmother to be in town to see her daughter graduate in a white coat and a pink rose, signing off as Dr Mallika.

Gayathri Ponvannan

5

LEARNING
EXPERIENCES

*Diagnosis is not the end, but the beginning
of practice.*

—Martin H. Fischer

An Eye for an Eye

Suraj had gone out to play that evening as he usually did every day after school. He fell down and hurt himself like he had several times before.

Or so he thought.

Back home, Shobha, his mother, saw his bruised elbow and frowned. 'Finish your milk,' she said, placing his glass on the edge of the table.

But Suraj simply sat there waiting for the milk; he could not see that side of the table. Something had pierced his eye and torn his iris, the shutter of our natural camera in the eye.

The seven-year-old was rushed to the emergency operation theatre of the hospital. The tear was sutured and his eye was bandaged, and everything seemed to be under control. Shobha spent the night by her son's bed, barely closing her eyes for a nap.

The next morning when the bandages were removed to inspect his eye, the doctor's expression became serious. The suture site was gaping, and there was high intra-ocular pressure in the eye ball. Shobha could not help but think of the beautiful drawings Suraj used to make as she wiped her tears and saw the little boy being wheeled into the operation theatre for the second time in less than twenty-four hours. Suraj was later discharged with half his field of vision and a prescription for over half a dozen medicines.

When I saw Suraj during the course of my ophthalmology case presentations in my third year of medical school, twenty days had passed since his surgery. His mother wept softly as she narrated the traumatic event that had brought her to the OPD that day. She told us everything, from the forgotten glass of milk to his love for drawing and that he had not even been going to school, let alone playing. I tried hard to not bite my lips when the brave little fighter told me with a straight face that he could not see a thing when I covered his left eye with my palm. I recalled the time when I was seven and being an accident-prone kid myself, I shuddered to think how I would have dealt with such an injury at that tender age, let alone now when I am twenty-two.

We took him to our teacher for the scheduled case presentation. Dr Ashok smiled at Suraj and talked to him before he looked at his prescription, a gesture not often shown by doctors who sit in OPDs that are jam-packed with patients and hundred other daunting responsibilities. More so in a government set-up like my college, where the lack of basic facilities has doctors at their wits' end. He listened to what the child and his mother had to say. At one point, he ruffled Suraj's hair and told him that he was a brave kid; it brought the hint of a much-needed smile to the boy's innocent face.

Dr Ashok wrote out the regimen for the medicines Suraj was supposed to take: a constellation of antibiotics and steroids, tablets and eye drops. He made sure Shobha could repeat the exact order and the frequency in which they had to be taken. He even arranged for some free medicines, aware of their economic condition, and made Suraj promise he'd be a good boy. This was done when he had at least fifty other restless patients in line and a group of novice medical students hovering over him.

Then he went on to take a brilliant class for us on ocular trauma and dealt with his other patients in much the same way.

It was the first time in my clinical experience that I saw a doctor putting so much of himself — his time and patience — to heal a person and not just treat the disease. It was my first example of clinical detachment coupled with a strange sense of attachment to human suffering. It is not always about saving lives; sometimes it is about providing a little quality to people's lives: a well-managed injury, relief from agonising pain, giving someone the power to see, telling a mother that her child would be just fine.

The class was informative, of course, but what I carried away was a lesson much deeper than medical science. I hope to remember this for as long as I can.

Suraj came back the following week and we examined him again. His right eye could now perceive light and he was slowly but surely on the road to recovery. Shobha went up to Dr Ashok, held his hand and repeated the instructions he had given her. She had diligently followed them for her child in the past one week.

Suraj saw the doctor smile at his mother in approval.

Sucheta Tiwari

Doctors in Bed

Watch a doctor writing a prescription: he's confident, gentle, and definite. If the patient opts for tablets instead of an injection, he will persuasively claim that 'it's just a little prick' and may also add, 'don't be such a coward'.

If a doctor happens to be on the receiving end, on a hospital bed in a patient's garb, sans the stiff white coat, wrapped up in a sheet in a hospital, he trembles at the sight of a nurse. Okay, not all of them behave the same way, but there are always exceptions. For some reason, doctors who lord over lesser mortals, fear side effects and risks of injections, capsules and scalpels far more than lay people. Do they trust other doctors to treat them without making mistakes?

One could do a thesis on the topic. I think what many of us forget, and sometimes doctors forget too, is that all of us are human, with our frailties and weaknesses, strengths and talents.

I remember one doctor who had undergone a kidney transplant. He'd been pragmatic and sensible throughout his ordeal. Until, post surgery, he was ready to go home. By all standards, that's a traumatic experience for the entire family. All patients who undergo this medical adventure ask many questions during the follow-up. Our doctor didn't, which is understandable, for even in the Internet era there are many questions left unanswered, but which people, especially technically-qualified persons, are hesitant to voice. Why? No one wants to be thought of as an ignoramus. A doctor asking another doctor what the former considers a 'stupid' or 'obvious' question can give rise to major embarrassment. Or so it is perceived. I've seen this happen with doctor patients who have come to check about cochlear implantation or some new remedies for ulcerative colitis.

There are also doctor moms who have no idea what to do when they've missed their children's inoculations and realised the error years later. There is panic and also hesitation to ask their colleagues for fear of ridicule or retribution.

The doctor who'd undergone the kidney transplant was petrified because he didn't know whether he could get back to his general family practice. What if he caught an infection? How would his patients react to his wearing a mask? I suggested he speak to the nephrologist and that I was the wrong person to advice him, but he turned down that offer. So miserable did he look that finally I told the nephrologist his patient's predicament and the situation was delicately handled.

Doctors hate it when they're told to 'lie still' or 'behave' when they're admitted as patients in the very hospital where they work. One highly qualified surgeon broke a limb whilst on a holiday. He flew down to his base and got an emergency surgery done. The very next day, he wished to get discharged, which was contrary to protocol. He ranted at the nurses for not obeying him. He raved at the junior doctors, saying, 'I'm occupying a valuable bed. There are other patients waiting for treatment. I need only rest, which I can give myself at home. You can't keep me here.'

When his secretary walked in, she was treated to a piece of his mind that left her in tears. It was a weekend and no one wanted to disturb the consultant in charge of admissions. The irony was that we weren't willing to give the latter's mobile number to him as per the rules of our hospital, though we all knew they were friends. A near-tantrum followed about how bureaucratic we were, and how stupid. Finally, we gave in, spoke to the admitting doctor and let our patient 'out'.

Doctors undergoing surgeries pray harder than any lay patient. Why do they always remember only the risks? It's a mystery to me.

I remember a dear old doctor, who saw ants on the ceiling when she was lying down in the ICU. She refused to believe she was hallucinating. 'I can see them,' she roared. 'It's useless telling you anything. Get so-and-so.' Who'd tell her she was imagining them? No one wanted to hurt her. She was so particular about infection control and physiotherapy that her bedside had become almost like a classroom, with her lecturing all and sundry on these topics and their importance.

If doctors make bad patients, relatives of doctors are much worse: 'Don't you think you should give me pantocid before this dose?' Or, 'My father was a surgeon, I know all about these things.' Try telling a senior cardiac doctor that he mustn't have extra salt in his soup when he's recovering from a bout of high blood pressure; if he wants it, that's it. The dietician isn't going to have her way. Tough old matrons are the only creatures on this planet who can handle him, besides possibly his own mother.

Young medics who join in to do a post-graduation course swagger in, for they are doctors, right? A couple of months and several mistakes later, after they've been yelled at by their seniors and verbally walloped by relatives, they succumb to their frights and humility takes over. (As an aside: I'd recommend a compulsory enema to hasten the process of sensitisation.)

Once they've got down to truly becoming professionals, they do get some divine properties. What about the greedy doctors you read about in the papers? Per one greedy soul, there are many, many more doing free or inexpensive treatment. So many delve into their own pockets to make sure the patient's treatment doesn't suffer for want of money, but their generosity isn't made public.

After ten years of interacting with patients and doctors, one thing I know for sure — an experienced Indian doctor, no matter what his field, is as good as if not better, than the best in the world. I'd trust him, or her, blindfolded.

Sheela Jaywant

He Taught Me Trust

It had been six months since I started my post-graduation. I had comfortably fit into the job of a first-year house surgeon, when Krishna Gameti, a young lad of about twenty-five years came with an admission slip in his hand. He had a swelling under the base of the tongue — a ranula — and was to be operated the next morning by one of our senior faculty members.

I finished the preliminaries and entered his name in the operation theatre list. I was to assist my professors the next day. It was almost eleven in the night when I finished with the ward work and left for the P.G. Hostel.

Outside the ward, a villager came to me and held my hand — a short guy, with the typical Mewari head turban, his small eyes sparkling with life. I was taken aback, and looked at him with slight agitation. He simply folded his hands, smiled and then told me that he was the father of Krishna Gameti. He asked me to assure him that everything would be alright the next day! I assured him that it was a routine surgery and there was nothing to worry about.

The next morning we had finished with six surgeries already by the time Krishna was laid on the operating table. Once he was knocked unconscious with drugs, I felt his pulse. There was no pulse! I nudged my professor's hand and informed him of my finding. He was ready with the knife and asked the anaesthetist to check. Then, he went ahead to cut open the ranula and our hearts sank! The blood that oozed out was dark instead of the cherry red that it should have been. The senior-most doctor shouted out that the blood was dark, and the anaesthetist shoved us away shouting, 'We don't have his heart! He is into a cardiac arrest!'

There was total panic in the OT, with all of us doing our bit to revive Krishna. After two minutes, we restored his heartbeat and we were all relieved; the surgery was deferred, and we waited for him to come around.

Unfortunately, his heart had stopped long enough to cause severe brain damage due to lack of oxygen. After two hours, despite infusing him with all kinds of drugs and oxygen, Krishna did not regain consciousness, though his vital body organs had started functioning independently. Krishna was shifted to the ward in that condition. He was alive, but his brain had been damaged. Now, it was a waiting game for us ... many a time, the brain recovers from such hypoxic events although the time of recovery cannot be predicted. We had to keep him alive till his brain came back.

I remember his father's face as I rushed alongside the

trolley to the ward carrying Krishna. He looked into my eyes and instinctively knew that something had gone wrong and then he folded his hands in complete reverence to me. That is one image I will carry to my grave — his helplessness, his surrender, and his pain. He raised his folded hands to his forehead, as if in front of a god. I was so struck by that gesture ... and felt so frustrated with my inability to reverse the events in the OT on that fateful day. I felt so small, so unworthy of his trust in me; I just lowered my gaze and kept walking alongside the trolley.

Day by day, his degree of consciousness deteriorated, and we helplessly watched him slip out of our hands. His father would just carry out our instructions day and night; he would bring the medicines as instructed to him, silently taking care of his son.

One day, while doing a routine check on him, I noticed a bed sore on his lower back. The first thing that came to my mind was to arrange for a water bed for Krishna. After a day of haggling with the bureaucracy, I finally managed to procure a water bed for him. I remember the trip we had to make to get that bed in an ambulance, carry it to the ward and then fill it up bucket by bucket. Finally, we put him on the water bed.

Then one day, the nursing staff told me that Krishna had not passed stools for the last three days. We got a surgical referral and they gave some kind of enema to him, but to no avail. Finally, I got a call from the surgical ward that somebody would have to carry out a finger evacuation of his fecal matter. I realised I had to take the initiative. That day, when I was going back to my room in the hostel, Krishna's father approached me with folded hands and fell at my feet. I was not prepared for this. I picked him up, his lips were quivering and tears were rolling down his cheeks as he said, 'Doctor! Whether my son is saved or not I will be always obliged to you, I will never forget what you have done for me, you are the incarnation of Lord Krishna for me.'

Exactly one month after his fateful arrest, Krishna developed seizures and went into decelerate rigidity, which was the beginning of the end. I asked the nursing staff to inform his father and other attendants of the impending end. I sat in my chair in the ward parallel to the prostrate body of Krishna, watching it go into rigors time and again.

I recollected that Krishna's father used to go to a nearby Shiva temple and I jumped out from the window of the ward and set out to look for him. There, under a neem tree, I saw his small frame, his head sunk between his folded legs. I walked up to him and stood there, waiting for him to look up. After a moment, he looked up but there was no sadness on his face, a strange glow reflected from his face. I sat down beside him, immersed in regret and sadness. When I raised my head there was no one there.

I slowly walked back to the ward. Krishna's father, Mangu Ram, stood at the feet of his son's corpse, having one final conversation with his boy's mortal body. In spite of all my reservations about intruding into his personal moment, I walked up to him and stood there in silence. My eyes were overflowing with the emotion of the moment, and I said to the old man, 'I am sorry we could not save your son.'

What he said to me still echoes in my mind, 'No, Dac saab, his time had come, this is the leela of the Saanwara (Lord Krishna). You have served him like a brother and I am a witness to it.'

Dr Omendra Ratnu
(As told to Shreeja Mohatta Jhawar)

His Miracle

Diabetes is a disease that sometimes affects people with such cruelty, it can send the patient into depression. Working as a part of the diabetic foot care team in my hospital, I often find myself lost, thinking about how an amputee and his family cope with the situation.

I had a case of limb salvage, where the patient was only thirty-five years old with severe left leg necrotising fascitis, nearly extending up to his knees. He also had chronic kidney failure that made him dialysis dependent. When he came to us, he was in sepsis and his kidneys had nearly shut down. He was immediately taken for dialysis, followed by an emergency debridement. The only person I saw with him during his entire treatment process was his wife.

His wife had been taking care of him for the past eight years as his kidneys had failed early in life. She had been the bread-winner for the family ever since. She did the household chores, looked after her husband and daughter, and worked as a maid.

His recurrent leg infections scared her. 'I don't want to think of the worst, Doctor, because I see nothing in my life without him; he is my strength,' she would say, although I believed it was the other way round.

Even after the surgery, her husband had to undergo multiple dialysis and daily dressings for the huge wound. This was draining her out financially, physically and mentally, but she never gave up. Her dedication towards her husband moved our entire team and we persuaded the hospital to waive most of the charges.

It has been three months since he got discharged. His wound had started to heal well, and each time his wife comes with him for a follow-up, she thanks our team profusely.

But we believe that it was more than just medicines that has cured this man; it was his wife's will power and strength to stand by him, giving him courage at each step and belief that he would make it.

As a doctor I would say, 'It wasn't the medicines, she was his messiah!'

Dr Sangeetha P. Sukumar

Indelible

Our lives as doctors are filled with a lot of stress that comes with long, erratic hours, anxiety for patients and the occasional disillusionment. The ability to cure a patient is always an achievement; each accomplishment gives us the same sense of fulfilment and motivates us to move on.

In 1978, I was working as a junior resident and was posted in the Casualty department of the medical college hospital in Kanpur. One evening, Rita, a twenty-six-year-old, was brought in a state of breathlessness. She was blue due to lack of oxygen and the initial X-ray showed extensive lung damage. She had a short history of fever and chest pain.

Rita was sinking rapidly and her breathing was getting more laboured by the minute. Ultimately, she lost consciousness and stopped breathing. There was no pulse or blood pressure and within minutes she went into respiratory arrest followed by cardiac arrest. Rita's heart had stopped.

I had already given her high doses of potent antibiotics, steroids and other supportive medication along with the oxygen, but there was no change in her condition. Within a few minutes, Rita's pupils had dilated and she was clinically dead. I started mechanical cardio-respiratory revival and asked my colleagues to help. The senior resident thought that the exercise was futile as cardiac arrest usually leads to death within a few minutes, but my instincts prompted me to keep trying. My determination to continue the process defied logic as plausibly it is not possible to revive a person after so much time has elapsed. Loss of blood flow to the brain causes irreparable damage or death.

After about twenty-five minutes of cardio-respiratory resuscitation, Rita's pupils began to react and in another ten minutes her pulse and spontaneous breathing had returned. During the next three days, Rita had two minor episodes of respiratory arrest but eventually she made a complete recovery. Rita went back to her job at the Reserve Bank of India, Kanpur, in less than two months after her clinical death.

This incident remains indelible in my mind. It was one of the greatest feats of my career and gave me the confidence and grit to always fight till the last. But our days are dotted with several small experiences as well which may seem trivial when compared to the major ones, but play an important role in lifting our spirits.

During my MBBS internship in Kanpur, all the young interns had a mandatory weekly rural posting; that is, we had to go to the villages in Uttar Pradesh, and these visits were eye-openers, as we witnessed how the poorest of the poor lived. Most of the patients lived in unhygienic and appalling conditions which gave rise to many health problems.

An old man in his eighties, suffering from severe chest infection that was not getting cured by the local quack, visited me. I gave him the regular medication and he was cured by his second visit.

He visited me again the next week, this time to convey his thanks. He smiled his toothless smile and urged me to accept the 'payment' along with his gratitude. He pushed something into my hand under the table. It was a small radish and a guava!

In over thirty years of practice, I cannot recall anyone rendering a more touching and meaningful payment for my medical services!

Dr S.C. Jain
(As told to Shreya Jain)

Of Compassion and Empathy

As a young girl, I first came across the image of the All India Institute of Medical Sciences (AIIMS) in 1984 when India's then prime minister Indira Gandhi was rushed to the country's premier medical institute after being shot. Years later, it was a heady feeling to walk into the same magnificent campus of AIIMS as a young journalist in search of a story. Doing a good story on health can give you a real high — they say politics changes the life of a nation but there's no doubt that health can change a person's life.

On a mild autumn evening, I had gone to AIIMS with one of my colleagues as we were doing a feature story on the growing cases of depression in urban India. As part of our work, we were supposed to interview doctors to understand the different case studies of depression. As per the appointment, we went to the department of psychiatry to meet the doctor. With great patience, the doctor explained to us about depression and its symptoms. He was very lucid. This was at a time when Google search was unheard of; researching a subject usually meant spending hours in the library or talking to experts.

Even as the doctor was explaining how difficult it is to cope with depression, he said there are some instances when the person suffering from depression makes it difficult for people who are taking care of them. Behaving like immature and irreverent souls, my colleague made the comment, 'Oh! Those persons are not really depressed but quite chalu (clever) actually. How can they make things difficult at home?'

The doctor looked quite shocked at first but then with a sense of calmness, said, 'I know you are very young. But as journalists don't be judgmental and don't jump to conclusions.' He advised us not to be brazen in life and develop a sense of compassion and empathy not only as journalists but as human beings. He said doing a story only for a byline should not be our sole goal in life, and we must take care to be sensitive to people and situations.

We were quite ashamed of our juvenile behaviour that autumn evening. Both of us didn't speak a word as we took the DTC bus back to office. But there was enough to guide us in our journey in life from then on. Those wise words of the doctor have always stayed with me. And that advice to have a sense of compassion and empathy has always helped me to evolve both in my professional and personal life.

Deepika

Selfless Love

In December 1994, I graduated as a doctor and went for my first job interview. I was assigned as a House Surgeon in the Burns Ward of the government hospital for the next six months. My friend, Ria, was also posted with me. In the welcome address, our Unit-in-Charge informed us authoritatively, 'Don't ever get emotionally involved with your charge. They are your patients only.'

There was a brigade of doctors, nurses and nursing orderlies to manage the huge ward. It was a difficult place to work — all patients came to the ward in extreme anguish, howling in pain. The dressing area always smelt of disinfectant.

Most of the patients there belonged to the lower socio-economic status and could not afford the fees in fancy hospitals. I was assigned to the female section of the ward, where many patients were dowry victims and their harrowing tales put humanity to shame. Many young, beautiful girls who had sustained life-threatening burns of more than seventy per cent were left there by their family members to die. Sometimes even their bodies were not claimed.

One morning, a patient named Savita was rolled in; she had sustained forty-five per cent burns while working in the kitchen. 'Another dowry victim,' I thought. No sooner had I finished my examination that her husband, Ram Swaroop, came to me and said, 'Doctor didi, please save my wife.'

'We are trying our best,' I gave my standard reply. 'Rascals, first they burn their wives and then they want us to save them,' I muttered to Ria.

'Come on, don't be emotional. Let's go for coffee,' replied my friend.

Savita managed to survive the critical phase. Her husband would come every day. Whenever we wrote a prescription for any drug, he would promptly get it. After a week, she developed fever, the sign of an infection setting in. After a swab was taken from the infected wound and sent for routine culture and sensitivity, her worried husband came to me.

'We have sent the swab and appropriate antibiotics will be started soon,' I said to dismiss him. He kept standing there, the pleading in his eyes apparent.

'Do you have any children?' I asked out of curiosity.

'No Madam, she has been treated but she cannot bear children,' he replied and left.

Two days later her report came — the diagnosis was 'pseudomonas areruginosa isolated'. She was resistant to all antibiotics except a new one, and her fever was still high. The Unit-in-Charge told us to start the patient on this new antibiotic but it was not available in the hospital pharmacy.

'Ask the patient's relative to get it,' ordered our Unit-in-Charge. Promptly the antibiotic prescription was handed over to Ram Swaroop. After a while he came back with a single vial of the drug.

'Ram Swaroop, she will need three such vials each day for at least seven days. You should have got at least ten vials,' I scolded him

'Doctor, you please give this. I will get the rest soon,' he assured me.

The dose was administered to the patient, who continued to deteriorate. Two days passed; Savita's husband kept arranging the vial in one or two batches.

Savita began to show signs of improvement. One morning Ram Swaroop came in without the vial. I yelled at him to get all the vials in advance or shift the patient to some other hospital. He did not reply and went away. Later, on my way out of the ward, I heard someone sobbing. It was Ram Swaroop.

'What happened?' I enquired.

'Doctor didi. I don't know what to do. I have sold everything I had including the utensils at home. My shop has closed down and there is no money left now. Each vial costs around three hundred rupees. I have also donated blood twice to earn some money. Now I have nothing. Please save her, I cannot live without her.' Saying this, he fell at my feet. I was completely taken aback — that day I realised that a prescription can cost somebody a lifetime of savings.

Next morning I arranged for some antibiotics through my medical representative friends. My friends and I also contributed whatever little we could from our paltry salary. 'I have to save her at all cost,' I told Ria.

Savita's condition gradually improved and she was ready

to be discharged after a few days. Ram Swaroop thanked me profusely.

'I have not done anything, Ram Swaroop. It is your love which has brought her back to you,' I replied.

Savita has suffered from small pox in her childhood and it had left her blind. Her face was completely scarred and also, she could not bear any children. I had seen young men bringing in their wives — beautiful young girls, recently married — who had been burnt for dowry. Many of them left the hospital never to return. I had heard fathers of young daughters saying 'who is going to marry her now with a burnt face'. And here was a man who had sold off everything he had, to save his love.

This incident left a big impact on my life; it taught me that to be a doctor you have to be a human first. Most doctors get free samples of drugs. Instead of passing them on to their friends who can very well afford them, they can give it to someone who actually needs it. It is easy to give a little when you have a lot, but to give away everything you have takes a lot of courage and that is the miracle of selfless love.

Dr Sonal Saxena

The Other Side

I was a robust young man, thirty-two-years old and doing well in life. My practice as a paediatrician was well established, I had just bought my first car, and life was good. I had worked pretty hard to achieve my standing as one of the better doctors of my town. I worked on Sundays and holidays, never turned down an emergency and worked unearthly hours. I did not slow down even when fatigued or sick; I simply popped a painkiller and carried on.

I still remember that fateful morning very clearly. I had woken up at 4 a.m. with severe pain in my neck. I was feeling slightly disoriented and the pain was unbearable. I called up a fellow physician and asked for advice.

'If the pain is unbearable, take an analgesic. I'll send over a nurse to give you the injection and we'll get you investigated in the morning,' he advised. The nurse came and gave me the injection, and within a few minutes I was half asleep as the pain subsided a bit. I decided to rest until morning in the hope that I would be fine when I woke up.

When I woke up some two hours later, I realised that my

right hand and leg were completely paralysed and I could not move them. Now that triggered off a major alarm and a lot of doctor friends descended, examined me and tried to reach a diagnosis. On failing to reach a consensus, they decided that I would be better off in a hospital. So I was bundled into a wheelchair and we caught the next train to New Delhi.

We reached in the evening and made our way to GB Pant Hospital. As we reached late, none of the consultants were available. However, the resident on duty admitted me and assigned me a bed in the general ward as there was a month-long waiting list for the private rooms. Those were the days before five-star private healthcare establishments had flooded the country.

I had virtually grown up in those surroundings as most of my life had been spent working in government hospitals; first as a student, then as a trainee and later as a consultant. But for the first time in my life, I found myself on the other side of the divide. The ward was dirty, the toilets reeked, and all the beds were occupied by patients in even worse condition than me. That was the longest night of my life. I could not sleep as I did not know whether I would ever be able to stand or walk again. Frightening visions of dreadful diseases like cancer, nerve degeneration and other unknown entities kept playing in my mind.

My miserable night passed and the morning brought in hope in the form of Dr A.K. Singh, the Professor of Neurosurgery. The whole day was taken up by extensive investigations, and in the evening I was taken to his office on a wheelchair.

'Vivek, I have studied your case in detail, and frankly, it is confusing. Your paralysis is due to a lesion in the neck. The

MRI has revealed a fluid collection in the cervical spine which is pressing on the spinal cord. The radiologist suggests a possibility of tuberculosis but I am not convinced.

'We have two options; we either put you on anti-tubercular drugs or open up your spine to see what the problem is. If required, we may even take a biopsy during the surgery. If you wish, you may go in for a second opinion,' Dr Singh said.

'Sir, what would you suggest?' I asked.

'Given a free hand, I would do a laminectomy and take a look. The fluid collection at that place is odd and something tells me it is not TB. But opening the cervical spine is a tricky business and there is always the possibility of complications. Why don't you take a second opinion?'

It was then that I made the most important decision of my life.

'Sir, I have full faith in you. Go ahead with the surgery.' The good doctor was still hesitant, but I simply reiterated my faith in him and God, and asked him to go ahead.

Next afternoon I was wheeled into the operation theatre. As the anaesthetist started the pre-operative drugs, I had a sudden panic attack. 'I am not getting out of here alive,' the thought which was at the back of my mind came to the fore with a blinding flash. However, I managed to hold on to my faith. The drugs took hold and I slipped into oblivion.

I woke up after a few hours. I realised two things: first, I was still in the realm of the living, and second, I had not been shifted out of the operation theatre. I saw an unknown face peering at me.

'I am the anaesthetist and was waiting for you to come around. I will now shift you to the recovery room.' I was anxious until Dr Singh visited me in a while and clarified that all the symptoms were caused by a simple clot of blood and there was no evidence of any other pathology. I walked out of the hospital a week later and have been absolutely normal for the last fifteen years.

Later, I realised that all the analgesics I had been taking on and off had probably precipitated the blood clot. I have forgotten the suffering, the mental and physical anguish and the feeling of helplessness and hopelessness of those days, but not the lessons learnt from the episode.

The suffering has made me a better human being and a better doctor. Now I know how it feels to be on the other side. I realise that however bad things may seem at a particular point of time, tomorrow is always better. Now the motto of my life is, 'This too, shall pass'.

I understand that one must always keep faith in the doctor who is treating you and in God. Now instead of offering sympathy to my patients and their parents, I give them empathy. Lastly, since that day I have never abused analgesics or overprescribed them to my patients.

Dr Vivek Banerjee

The True Healer

A doctor always dreads treating patients belonging to their own family. His fears are further heightened if this person happens to be his own child. Am I competent enough? Am I on the right path? These are some of the questions that crowd his mind, causing him great worry and torment. It happened in the 1950s to my father who was a general physician. He was not only a knowledgeable man, but also hardworking and dedicated to his profession. People flocked to him for relief and advice at all times of the day; it brought him satisfaction as well as confidence.

Then came the day when he was thrown into a situation that he would later describe as the toughest journey he had experienced as a doctor.

The entire family had gone to a relative's house for a wedding. The approach was through a narrow lane, lined on either side by tall trees and bushes. While returning, my brother Lakshman, who was then ten years old, let out a cry of pain. Something had stung him on his right ankle. Fortunately it was not a snake but he was in great pain and had to be helped into the car.

On reaching home, Father took a look at it. Two red marks, the size of pin-pricks, were visible. He applied some healing ointments but it did not relieve the pain or the swelling. Lakshman hardly slept that night, and by morning the entire foot was swollen.

Poultices were applied and tablets given, but none of them brought any relief; soon the area turned into an open wound. Father called in his colleagues, but none were able to help. They were all of the opinion that little else could be done. Father now turned to Ayurvedic treatment. The wound was bathed in many different oils. The pain was excruciating, but no perceptible difference was seen.

Days passed and the wound began to go deeper. It was feared that gangrene would set in; my brother was in danger of losing his foot. He had not been attending school for three months and had become listless and cranky because of this whole episode.

My grandmother, although not a great believer in astrologers, decided to consult one. He did his calculations and suggested that a chicken be sacrificed. When she conveyed this to my father, he came up with a reply that made an indelible imprint on my mind.

'How can you save one life by taking another?'

We seemed to have reached a dead end. It is said that when all doors are closed, God opens a window. A doctor friend, who had just returned from abroad, examined my brother.

'The treatment so far has been conventional and somewhat

invasive. Just leave it alone. Bandage the foot lightly. Keep it clean and leave it to nature. It will heal,' he advised.

My father followed his suggestion and gradually we began to perceive a difference. Progressively, the wound got better and healed. The pain too decreased and eventually my brother was able to walk and even run. Apart from losing a little strength in the foot, he regained his health completely.

My father regarded this episode as a great learning experience. Amongst other things, it made him look upon himself as a facilitator rather than a healer. He was able to empathise with his patients even more. Most of all, his belief that nature is the greatest healer was strengthened. He always believed, 'A doctor treats, it is God who heals.'

Leela Ramaswamy

Two-minute Consultation

After years of medical training and working at Yale University in the United States, I returned to treat patients in India. The week after I joined work, I was told by the Head of the Department that I was spending too much time with each patient; Indian patients unlike their American counterparts did not need so much explanation, he said I was told to just tell them what to do and that was it. I shouldn't take more than two minutes for each consultation.

That week a family from West Bengal visited me with their child, who had a hole in the heart and needed surgery. I aimed for my two-minute consultation and said, 'Your child has a hole in the heart, we need to operate. It is a very high-risk operation. I am giving you a letter ... you can go to Room No. 4 and get the child admitted.' They sat at the other end of my consultation table, speechless. I repeated what I had said and they quietly left the room.

Two days later as I was getting into my car to go home, I saw the same family sitting near the hospital entrance, crying.

'What happened?' I asked gently. 'Did you not get her admitted? Can I help in any way?'

The sympathy in my voice gave the father the courage to speak. 'We are from a small village near Kolkata. We were unable to have children for fifteen years until, finally, God gave us this little baby girl. But she has been sick since she was born. She has been on medication for the past three years but nothing has worked.

'This is the first time someone has told us that she has a hole in her heart. What is that? How serious is this operation? We have decided that if she needs it, we will certainly get it done. We have no money but we have a small plot of land on which we grow carrots. We sell those carrots to make a living. I can sell that land to get money for this operation. But what if even that amount is not enough? What will we do then? But more importantly Doctor, you said "high risk" ... can you guarantee that she will survive the operation? After fifteen years, God sent Pinky to us and we cannot believe He would want to take her back so soon. Doctor, are you sure she needs this operation? Will she be okay after it?'

I stood there feeling dazed. How lightly I had told them that their lovely Pinky needed a high-risk operation. I had never imagined that they did not know about her heart condition, and that she had been born after years of prayers. They would need to sell their only source of income to fix her heart, and then they would have a healed heart but no food.

If I had known all this would I have stated the facts of the case differently? Would I have been gentler? Would I have spent more than two minutes? Would I have offered to help them raise the funds for the operation so they could keep their land? Would I have reassured them so that they would not be sitting here full of despair and crying?

I could never quite undo the damage I had done to them, but what I knew for sure was that I would listen, reassure and give each of my patients the time needed to clarify their doubts and pour out their hearts. There would never be a two-minute consultation for me again!

Dr Sunita Maheshwari

When Patients are Teachers

I once read in a magazine that in some eastern country, the cadavers which are dissected to study anatomy are revered as teachers. The students are expected to find out all they can about who that person was, what he did, and after the lessons are over, they respectfully put flowers on the body in gratitude.

What I do know is that there is a lot one can learn from patients and their visitors. They think so differently from the doctors, nurses and other staff at the hospital. It's interesting to know their points of view at times.

I used to organise awareness programmes on various issues like organ transplantation, etc., to people who came for their health check-up. I used to talk about how our eyes, kidneys, heart and liver could be donated after death, even if the patient was brain dead. We discussed the difference between brain death, cardiac death and coma, between a liver and a cadaver donor. After the session, I would deal with the questions.

'If we donate our heart, then will all our memories get transferred to the recipient?'

'Will our likes and desires get transferred?'

'Can we buy a cadaver?'

My favourite was, 'If we have a funeral without the kidneys, then in the next life will we be born without any ...'

No one thinks of this when they get their teeth removed, or cut their hair and nails, or when they have to get rid of their troublesome appendix or uterus. 'Beta,' one elderly lady counselled me, 'don't get involved in talking about such things, you will suffer.'

'How?' I asked.

'You will die,' she said. Considering that all of us must one day perish, that wasn't a revelation.

People are always talking to one another especially outside a clinic, when they are waiting in queues or in the waiting areas of ICUs or wards. I have heard people sitting around in the hospital corridors chatting and exchanging symptoms, real or imaginary, comparing their 'sugar' with others. Many visitors love to show off how sick they are rather than talk about the patient who's actually been admitted. Some claim they have heart problems, while others have different kinds of illnesses.

Some time ago I remember seeing a child make his biscuit soggy with his saliva and then rub it on the arm of a chair, and on seeing this, the mother walloped him. Someone watching the episode counselled the mother to be patient while telling her that children that age did naughty things. Minutes later, the child went and wiped his mouth on that very person's trouser. There was silence all around. This time the mother said nothing and neither did the stranger. The child continued with his pranks, and no one else gave any more advice on how to tackle a truant child.

Doctors habitually come late and waiting areas are great levellers and platforms for forging friendships. I remember two ladies whose mothers or mothers-in-law were admitted in the ICU. These ladies got chatting and within a day they were discussing their likes and dislikes, the traits of their respective communities, and which one was fond of food. The winner was the one who remarked: 'Even our sari borders have pineapples, mangoes and fish on them. No parrots, peacocks or flowers, you see?'

The ICU visitors' areas bring about an intimacy that possibly only a full day's cross-country second-class train travel might. I learnt that stress can be handled in various ways and even life and death situations can be taken in one's stride when people share their feelings. When people share sorrow I have seen it bring comfort. On one occasion, when a family had run into financial difficulties because of the medical expenses the others present donated a sum to tide over the period so that the treatment could continue without further tension.

The OPD section has its own share of stories. One incident I remember was how a villager had got his stool sample in a shoe box lined with aluminum foil. He then tried to convince the girl at the counter that his was the best method to collect and transport that precious cargo. Of course it was precious, for the tests done on it would determine the course of treatment and his future health condition!

Another time it was a devoted wife who stood outside the restroom holding her husband's clothes and instructing him how to use Anne French to remove the hair on his chest for a stress test. These things taught us how awkward certain situations can be for a person who has come to get some tests done, and how innovatively people tackle the barriers they come across. Every episode teaches us something new about ourselves.

When we see patients in intense pain, at the end of their life, or maybe facing a lifetime of debilitation or disability, they make us think about our life. There are some patients who overcome their illness miraculously, defy the doctor's prognosis; these are the ones who are looked upon with wonder and respect. But there are others who, with everything going right, take a turn for the worse inexplicably and despite best efforts, just quit on life: they teach us something too ... that life is unpredictable, that science and the human mind has its limitations.

In addition to all of this, there are arrogant fresh medical graduates who enter the world of post-graduation and believe they know it all in just a couple of months or even less. They learn slowly over a period, through mistakes and exposure to different situations, and from the guidance of their superiors, that they need to be patient and attentive while listening to their patients.

An example that comes to mind is that of a woman who had both her knees replaced, but refused to go home because she complained her back was paining. The physiotherapist said she wasn't co-operating and needed to exercise. The surgeon was annoyed because in spite of a successful surgery and no infection or post-operative problems, she was not walking even after a month. Finally, out of sheer irritation, he got an MRI done on her, and the results showed TB of the spine.

Quite often people refuse to allow post-mortem to be done on patients who have died of unknown causes — what they often don't realise is that's the only way doctors can learn more and save more lives.

For a doctor, there's no teacher like a patient, dead or alive.

Sheela Jaywant

Words From a Stranger

It's strange how sometimes one learns the most important lessons of life from a person one hardly knows. Words that change our lives are sometimes spoken by people who did not even exist in our universe some time back.

In a doctor's profession, one comes across people from all spheres of life on a daily basis. A unique relationship is established between a patient and a doctor, which at times cannot be defined. They sometimes share more with each other than they do with their friends or relatives.

It was a Tuesday. I remember because Mohan used to visit me every Tuesday. He would sometimes visit as a patient but most times as a friend. That day he came with another friend Ram, a young man with a face that looked too old for his age. After talking for a while, I learnt that Ram had been fighting cancer for the past two years. Now you may imagine a sick young boy with no zest for life, someone who is tired of fighting. But Ram was totally different — he was more alive than any of us perfectly healthy people.

I could not hold back my thoughts anymore and asked him

the secret behind the adrenaline rush he seemed to possess at all times. He said, 'Doctor Saahab, you save lives, but you don't know its worth yourself?'

I was stunned at his rebuke, as he continued, 'Life is like a rose. Sure it has its thorns, but you need to ignore the thorns and look at its beauty. The beauty lies in the details. It is better adored and enjoyed when it's blooming, because it has a short lifespan. Soon its beauty will wither and become lifeless. It will all come to an end.'

These words, coming from the mouth of a cancer patient in his twenties, made me feel so small. I will never forget the sparkle, the ray of hope in his eyes that reflected his faith in the words he had just uttered.

From that day on, I started treating life as a gift, as a delicate rose.

In fact, I hope everyone who reads this story believes in it too.

Life is too short to complain about or be unhappy. We ought to enjoy it till it lasts because it will be taken away, just like a gush of wind reduces the beautiful rose into nothingness.

Nikita Pancholi

6

MIRACLES DO HAPPEN

Miracles are not contrary to nature, but only contrary to what we know about nature.

—Saint Augustine

A Job Well Done

It was not so long ago when a qualified doctor was hard to find and a dedicated one, even more difficult. Government hospitals were set up in remote districts but were either short-staffed or run by people who cared least about their patients. The use of allopathic medicine had spread all over the country but it had yet to filter down to the small towns and villages. It was during such a time that my grandfather had the courage to pack his bags and move from the lush green fields of Malda in West Bengal to the sandy deserts of Sirohi in Rajasthan.

Dr Lahiri, my grandfather, never regretted his decision, despite the many changes he had to make in his lifestyle, one of them, of course, being the lack of a constant supply of fish! It was a small inconvenience compared to the love and respect that he received from the people of Abu Road, where he lived. No important decision was ever taken without him, be it on town planning or education. He seemed to have an omniscient status and everyone was willing to bend over backwards for him, for there were few lives there that he had not touched. I often basked in his reflected glory whenever I went to visit him in the summer holidays.

It was one such lazy Sunday afternoon when the door bell rang. A group of villagers, dressed in their traditional clothes, stood outside with their hands folded in gratitude. They had brought a couple of bags of wheat and several vegetables with them. My grandfather was a man of serious disposition, but there was a broad smile on his face as he looked at a young man who stood out from the crowd because of his western attire.

It took me down memory lane, to the heyday of 'Daktar Lehri's' career, when he was the only doctor in the entire district of Sirohi. One summer afternoon, while my grandfather was taking a nap, a large group of wailing villagers had landed at our doorstep. A man was carrying a boy in his arms, who was unconscious. My grandfather picked up the boy's hand to check his pulse. He held it for a long time, his forehead furrowed. The pulse was erratic and very weak. For a moment, he thought that they had lost the boy, Harish. Then he heard a faint pulse again. He looked up and told the father that he would try but could not promise anything. The father pleaded desperately; Harish was the only son in their large joint family and only Dr Lahiri could ensure the continuance of the family name.

Harish was taken into the outhouse that served as Dr Lahiri's dispensary at home. He immediately administered an injection and then called for cold water and ice to be brought to try and bring down the fever. Despite everything, the fever refused to subside. The typhus (cerebral meningitis) had wreaked havoc with the boy's system. Grandfather's dinner lay untouched as he sat attending the patient and my grandmother was asked repeatedly to refill the ice tray in the refrigerator.

Khichdi was prepared for the boy and his family. Though it was way past my bed time, nobody paid me any attention since everyone was deeply involved in tending to the boy. Grandfather had sent most of the relatives and villagers away from the room, and their sleeping arrangements were made on the porch. Laxman, the compounder, had been called and was now busy helping grandfather with wet pads of cold water. Four hours passed this way and we watched as another injection was administered. Mashed food and liquids were fed to the boy, but he would immediately throw up.

The boy's head and feet were bathed in ice cold water to bring down the temperature, while a drip was arranged and glucose, procured from the dispensary, was administered through the intravenous tube. There was an eerie calm around the patient as everyone sat and waited. When I awoke the next day, my grandfather was still sitting on his stool beside the boy, just as I had seen him the previous night. He smiled as he saw me and asked me to fetch him some water. I knew then that the worst was over.

Grandfather wanted to see the boy sitting up before he sent him back. He knew that once back in the village, neither would his medicines be given on time nor would there be any control over what the boy ate. On the third day, the boy sat up. The smile on grandfather's face said it all. There were no words needed to express his joy. The family left happily soon afterwards.

Dr Lahiri had won another battle against the dreaded disease. He never refrained from saying that Harish's recovery had been a miracle of sorts. Harish had been in that narrow realm between life and death when he was brought to him. There was little hope when he had administered that first injection, and he had in fact prayed to all the powers in the universe to help the boy. It must have been a truly benevolent God who had listened to his prayer, for Dr Lahiri was a man of science, who firmly believed that there were no miracles!

Today, Dr Lahiri is no longer alive but if you happen to visit Abu Road and ask for his address, anyone will be able to point you in the right direction.

Tulika Mukerjee Saha

Beyond Our Understanding

•

I saw him as a newborn, beautiful but blue baby. I put the echo probe on his chest and made the diagnosis — d-TGA (transposition of the great arteries). It was an easy diagnosis for me to make but a difficult one for his parents to deal with. The main blood vessels from his heart were mixed up because of which blue blood was going to his body and the red blood was going back to the lungs; it was essentially a fatal situation.

The only thing that could save him was a surgery, an arterial switch procedure wherein the main vessels would be cut and sutured back to the correct spots on the heart. It was a high risk operation; if it was successful he would live, if it wasn't he would die. If we didn't operate, he would die.

His parents wanted to do everything in their power to save his little life. They signed on the high risk consent form and he was wheeled in for an open heart surgery. Three weeks in the intensive care unit on the ventilator, on medications pumping his heart, on the latest treatment the world knew ... and he made it through. He was now a beautiful pink baby, back in his mother's arms.

I saw him in follow-up treatment sessions as he grew into a lovable five-year-old with sparkling eyes and red cheeks. His parents were happy and grateful. At times like these it really felt worthwhile to be a doctor.

One day, just before his sixth birthday, he walked into my clinic for a routine check-up. I looked at the ECG and was puzzled; he seemed to have developed a complete heart block. It was highly unusual for such a development to occur so many years after his surgery. I did some further testing and came to the conclusion that however abnormal it may be, he needed a pacemaker implanted urgently.

His parents were shell-shocked, unable to comprehend what was happening. Their healthy child had been through the worst that a baby could go through, and had yet survived ... and now I was looking them in the eye and telling them that he needed a pacemaker, another huge surgery. He looked so normal and so healthy. They went home to think about it and never came back to see me.

Six months later the shrill ring of my cell phone pierced through the blasts of firecrackers on Diwali night. It was his mother crying. Their boy had stopped breathing! I left the Diwali celebrations at home and rushed to the hospital where they were waiting anxiously. But it was too late ... his heart had stopped beating even before he had reached the hospital.

His parents had hoped that I was wrong and had tried alternative medication instead. They were now drowned in grief and guilt. I spent the night with them, sedated his mother and told them that God found him beautiful and lovely, and thus had called him.

One year later, I saw a baby in my clinic, beautiful and pink. He was an exact image of the blue baby I had treated seven years back. Pushing him in his pram was the mother. We hugged and she told me that she had brought her new baby for a check up, to make sure his heart was okay. I commented on his uncanny resemblance to his older brother. And she said, 'Yes, Doctor, he cries like him and even behaves exactly like him. We believe it was true what you told us the night Anshul died — God loved Anshul and took him. But then he saw how unhappy we were and how much we missed him, so He sent him back to us in the form of Akash here.'

Dr Sunita Maheshwari

Every Day Holds the Possibility
of a Miracle

As an aesthetic surgeon, I have operated on many women, some who have been disfigured due to accidents or diseases and others who desire to look more aesthetically appealing. However, over a period of time, I have realised that their needs might be different, but their expectations from surgery are always the same — a more confident self and a fuller life. I feel worthy each day with the difference I make to human lives. Aesthetic surgery is an incredible art and it gives me an opportunity to create miracles through my profession. However, I had not actually realised this until I met Priya.

In the middle of an ugly divorce with her husband and trying to gain custody of her only child, Priya's life was at crossroads. One day, as she sat for her morning prayers, with shaken faith and a million complaints to God, she thought her life couldn't get any worse. After the prayer, as she lit a lamp at the altar and bowed her head in front of God, her sari caught fire. Numb with shock, her limbs froze and she couldn't react fast enough. Within ten minutes she had suffered major burns on her upper body.

And that's how she came to me — her entire upper body severely burnt. Her neck and hand movements were extremely restricted due to the burn scars. And, like all patients with a high degree of burns, her concern was whether she would ever be able to lead a normal life.

On examination, I found that the only way I could tackle this surgery was with artificial dermal skin, which is gene-modified tissue engineered skin. But it was a very complex procedure and her ordeal would extend into post-operative care. Prolonged discussions and a lot of explanations later, her big surgery was planned.

During the procedure to reconstruct such a large area, we used over nine hundred staples to make sure that the new skin did not shear and stayed in place. Through the entire process, Priya surprised us with her calm smiling face and the strength to bear pain when those staples were removed and the painful process of rehabilitation began.

She said to me, 'This incident was the turning point of my life. I don't complain to God anymore. I only marvel at how I am a living miracle and how much potential life holds.'

On her last day in the hospital, Priya narrated a deeply moving poem to me:

When somewhere within your heart a tempest rises,
And the tide of emotions takes you deep.
Let the calm of your soul nourish you,
And make your faith take a leap!

And as she prepared to take life's challenges head-on, Priya taught me the most important lesson of my life as a surgeon — every day holds the possibility of a miracle and the days when you succeed in creating one, are the most memorable days in your life.

Dr Sunil Choudhary

From the Diary of Dr Biswas

Dr Biswas was in a ruminative mood. We were chatting, when he started to relate a strange incident:

Many inexplicable events happen with a doctor as he practices. One evening, while I was driving home, suddenly a middle-aged, bearded man lurched in front of my car. Had I not applied the brakes on time, I would have crashed into him. However, though he was unhurt, he fell down. Immediately I got down from the car and rushed to him.

'Why were you crossing the road like a blind man?' Do you want to die?' I shouted at him.

His clothes were disheveled and he smelt of local alcohol. He tried to speak, but his speech was slurred. Seeing him unhurt and safe, I was about to return to my car when a woman's voice stopped me.

I turned and found a petite woman running towards me. She was in her mid-thirties, clad in an ordinary cotton sari.

'Sir,' she said. 'Thank you very much. You have saved his life.'

'Is he your husband?' I asked casually.

'Yes, Sir,' she replied, a bit fearfully. Most probably my formal dress and the stethoscope peeping out of my chest pocket made her look at me like that.

'Take care of him. Looks like he has had too much to drink,' I said.

'Are you a doctor?' she asked me.

'Yes, I am. Why?'

'He has a lot of medical problems, Sir. I want to consult a good doctor,' she said doubtfully as though she was not sure of herself.

She looked to be a woman of slender means and I knew well that she could not afford my consultation fee. Yet her simplicity caught my fancy. I gave her my business card.

'Thank you, Sir. We stay in that slum,' she said and indicated a small cluster of dingy houses on the other side of the street occupying the pavement.

As I started my car, I saw the woman helping her husband stand on his feet, scolding him. Once he stood she draped her arms around him and led him to their house. Looking at them pass by it occurred to me that the woman loved her husband a lot. I smiled, thinking she would probably never turn up with her husband.

However, soon she proved me wrong when, one evening, she came to my clinic with her husband.

Balkrishna was silent while his wife, Suruchi, talked at length, telling me that he often vomited blood. Sometimes, for days together, he slept continuously. He was an inveterate drunkard and it was the first time that she had managed to convince him to see a doctor.

I asked a few questions to the taciturn Balkrishna and suspected that his liver was partly damaged. Later medical tests proved my suspicion correct. I strictly told him to stop drinking and prescribed him some medicines.

I will not go into details; Balkrishna's condition deteriorated steadily. Though he did not visit me anymore, Suruchi continued coming to me twice or thrice a month. She could sense my affection for her and would tell me that Balkrishna always refused to take medicine, and beat her if she insisted. Every passing week made her more feeble and lifeless. Every time I talked to her, I would feel that she deserved a better husband.

One day I told her, 'Suruchi, why are you wasting your days with him? He ill-treats you. You are childless. You can easily leave him and start your life anew.'

She gave me a wry smile in response, and said, 'It would have been very easy to do, Sir. But I love him deeply. He may be an erring husband, but he gave me many beautiful years. I want to see him in better health only because I love him. I cannot desert him at any cost.'

Suruchi did not visit me nor did I see Balkrishna again for the next six months. One evening I bumped into Suruchi, and I was at a loss for words. Just a quick glance at her and I knew that she was a widow now. The mangalsutra around her neck was missing.

'Hello, Sir,' she greeted me in a calm voice.

'Hello Suruchi,' I said.

'He left me forever, Sir, about five months back. It was a peaceful death,' she said.

'I am sorry. I wish he had taken his medicines on time. Things would have been better,' I felt sorry for Suruchi although not for her husband.

'Why should you be sorry, Sir? He has left only his mortal

body, but otherwise he is always with me. Moreover, he is helping other people now with his divine power.'

Intrigued by her story I went with her to her place. On the way she narrated what had happened after his death. She was devastated for a few days; but one night she had a strange dream.

'At first, I did not understand the message he wanted to give me in my dream. But I followed his instructions. Within a few weeks I felt a strange transformation occurring in me. My neighbours could sense my transformation and gradually ...' Suruchi stopped as we reached her slum.

Curious, I followed Suruchi to her house and was startled to find no less than ten men and women sitting on a mat with their eyes closed as though they were meditating. In front of them on a straight-backed chair there was a framed photograph of Balkrishna and a water pot.

Pointing to the water pot, Suruchi told me, 'This water is blessed by him, Sir. That old aunty, sitting there, was suffering from osteoarthritis and could barely walk for the last many years. No medicine could help her. But this blessed water helped her recover completely. And that girl, Anita, could not conceive for many years. They consulted many doctors but to no avail; she got pregnant only after taking this elixir for no more than two weeks. The news spread around very fast and now many come and pray, sitting in front of his photograph.'

When the doctor concluded the narration, there was silence for some time, and then I suggested, 'Can we call it faith healing?'

'I do not know,' said the doctor philosophically.

Ratnadip Acharya

7

FUNNY TALES

I learned a long time ago that minor surgery is when they do the operation on someone else, not you.

—Bill Walton

A Brush with Doctors

Doctors! Well, I should know about them ... I have practically grown up with the rascals at the medical college where I studied. Yes, I too am a doctor, which is no big deal — until I got stuck on the other side of the table.

I had sustained a couple of serious injuries one after another. First I fractured my spine and then I managed to get a finger partially amputated. The fracture was treated by a classmate, a neurosurgeon called MS, while the plastic surgery for the chopped finger was done by another classmate, known as TR.

'How does it feel, getting treated by classmates?'

Well, I really do not know how to describe the feeling. The trust is implicit and there is also a sense of camaraderie. What is equally important is that one can actually relax with a doctor who has been your classmate at one point of time. One can even verbally abuse the doctor in the choicest of vernacular and get away with it unscathed — yeah, I suppose that is the real highlight of this relationship!

Friendly comradeship.

Not that they do not get back at you: I suppose, even a doctor looks forward to a situation where he can verbally abuse the patient without breaking the Hippocratic Oath. (You are absolutely right, we *are* a bunch of twisted halfwits from the best medical college that the country has to offer, or so says the *India Today* poll. I wonder if people from other colleges are less twisted.)

But to get back to the story — I arrive at the hospital for plastic surgery for my chopped index finger. TR calls out, looking up from his cup of steaming tea, 'Abey! Khali pet aaya hai na? (You've come with an empty stomach, no?).'

I look longingly at his tea before saying, 'Yes, I haven't had a drop of water since I woke up six hours ago.' He looks duly satisfied at the power he holds over me.

TR tries to look solicitous. 'Actually, this surgery requires a local anaesthesia. You can have a cup of tea ... it won't make a difference. I wouldn't have done it for a "normal" patient, but for a classmate, it's fine.'

I accept the tea gratefully, but only after asking if it is actually safe to do so. 'Of course it is safe. You think I would take even a minuscule risk with you? I am administering only local anaesthesia ...'

Convinced, I take a few sips before the OT assistant comes in and announces that the OT has been prepared for the surgery. I look longingly at the cup as I place it down, almost full, and troop behind TR into the operation theatre.

He injects the anaesthetic and proceeds to open the dressing that hides my grizzly looking stump. I let out a scream.

'Stop screaming, you moron!' he admonishes lovingly. 'I have already injected the anaesthesia. It is not hurting, you can just barely feel the touch.' He then proceeds to tug at the bandage, while lavishly pouring spirit and tincture on the wound.

'You moron!' I scream back just as lovingly. 'The damn lignocaine has not worked.' He stops.

'We'll wait for some time,' he says magnanimously.

'Abey, Looney ...' comes the cheerful voice of MS. Needless to say he has realised that I am being operated upon and has decided to pay me a social call — and what better place than the operation theatre. He slaps me on my shoulder, jarring the table and causing the IV line to shake a little.

'Ouch!' I scream as the needle jerks inside my vein and stimulates about a million nerve endings. 'Rags, throw this guy out of the OT.'

'Hah! High hopes,' says MS. 'You can't throw me out. Oh, hi!' he says as another classmate, an ophthalmologist, OP, strolls into the theatre.

TR has started hacking away again. I start screaming, while a whole crowd of people are trying to tell me not to be such a sissy. Gradually it dawns on them that, due to some quirk of physiology, local anaesthesia does not work on me!

The surgery is fairly complicated and will take about two-and-a-half hours — obviously, it would be a nightmare without anaesthesia. All my friends look at Rags, the anaesthetist. He casually mentions that he would now have to give me general anaesthesia. As he asks the assistant to load the medicines, he casually reconfirms if I am on an empty stomach. 'Actually, I had a few sips of tea just before entering the OT,' I inform him.

He shakes his head, 'Lona, how could you be so silly? I can't give you general anaesthesia after tea.'

The moron brigade has a quick conference. Obviously they couldn't leave the surgery half done and wait for another day. 'Abey, is it still paining?' TR asks, pinching my finger with a pair of forceps. It hurts a lot, though the pain is not as severe as it would have been if the anaesthesia had not worked at all — but why let them know?

'Oooh ... ow!' I howl.

MS steps forward and removes the blindfold, warning me not to look at my finger. 'Look at me. Scream as loud as you can.' Almost on cue, TR starts hacking away.

'Shut up. It's paining ... ooooh ... aaaah!!'

Over the next two hours, MS and OP proceed to tell me jokes, take photos and videos, transmit them on Facebook and show me responses from other classmates and even dance a jig.

Through this mayhem TR continues to diligently on restoring my chopped finger, while I carry on with a steady stream of abuse aimed at the plastic surgeon, neurosurgeon, ophthalmologist as well as a group of anaesthetists.

In the end, the operation was completed with 'vocal' rather than local anaesthesia. The finger healed beautifully (I typed out this story, didn't I?), the scar diminished and our friendship grew even stronger.

'Is it common to have such mayhem in the OT during an operation?'

'Is it common to see a senior acclaimed neurosurgeon (almost god to his patients) dancing a gig and getting abused for it?' The reply would most definitely be in the negative.

'How does it feel being treated by your own classmates?'

I don't know. What I do know is that I wouldn't have it any other way.

Lona

A Clinic with No Patients

My former classmate, Rahul, is a doctor now. He works as a private physician for a factory in the suburbs of Mumbai. A couple of years back, I met him in his clinic and he shared quite a few interesting stories about his patients.

'Ours is a free clinic,' Rahul told me. 'The factory management pays me well and I don't charge any consultation fee from these people. Even medicines are given free of charge.' I was surprised and said, 'They must really care for their staff to provide such an amazing service at no cost.'

'True. But guess what, when we started this clinic, people hardly ever came here,' he said. 'Initially we thought that the people were not aware of this free service. So we printed posters about the clinic, distributed colourful flyers showing the clinic's location, the various facilities available, and most importantly, we advertised the fact that all the services could be availed free of cost.

'In spite of our efforts, somehow people still didn't come to the clinic. It was as if they didn't want to get treated by me.

They just ignored me and my clinic. For many weeks I was sitting here all alone, worrying about losing my job.

'A couple of months later, I had gone to the factory to meet a supervisor. Right there, in front of my eyes, a young worker got injured due to a careless mistake. Fortunately, it did not seem to be an emergency but at the same time I knew that he needed first aid urgently.

'So I asked the other workers to bring him to the clinic. I, too, accompanied them; after all he was going to be my first patient and I didn't want to miss the chance of treating him. Who knows, this might help break the ice and make all other workers use the clinic!

'After a few minutes, we reached the clinic. I used all possible medicines to do an elaborate first aid treatment. Within a couple of hours, the young man was back to his normal self, smiling and cracking jokes. I too felt very relieved.

'When it was time for him to leave, he thanked me and asked me how much was the fee. I was waiting precisely for that moment and, in the most dramatic way possible, I announced that he need not pay a paisa. "It's all free, courtesy the factory management," I replied.

'But he refused to accept that. He insisted repeatedly that I should charge him a fee. To that I replied that it was against the rules to charge him a fee.

'That's when he told me, "Doctorji, if I don't pay for this treatment, I won't get cured. That's what my mother has always told me." That's when it struck me. Aha! Looks like the people in this region have this belief that free treatment won't cure them. That's why no one has turned up in our clinic. This young chap had solved this mystery for me.'

I had been listening to the story with keen interest, and asked Rahul, 'So how did you solve the problem?'

'Simple. I narrated the incident to our management and requested them to collect a token fee of just one rupee for treatment and medicines. They agreed and we implemented the new rule immediately. Within the next couple of days, the workers and their family members started visiting our clinic. They paid that one rupee with the utmost satisfaction and went back with the assurance that it would cure them.'

Finally, Rahul finished his story with the statement: 'After all, a doctor can only do his best; the other fifty per cent is purely in the minds of the patients. First, that needs to be taken care of, to ensure a complete cure!'

N. Chokkan

A Unique Patient

During the early Seventies, I was the only dentist in a small town in the south of Maharashtra, and had quite a busy practice. It was around 8 p.m. on a Saturday evening when I spotted a man dressed somewhat strangely waiting in my clinic. He looked like a farmer, and was wearing a dirty white sadara with ankle-length pajamas. He looked tired, yet there was a sparkle in his eyes that was unmistakable.

I was curious when he passed his turn to two other patients who had arrived after him. He kept on waiting, and when I enquired about this peculiar behaviour, he mentioned that he would consult me only after I was done with all the other patients for the day.

That was strange, I thought. Finally when he came in, I asked him what was wrong with his teeth. He was shy at first, then started apologising and said he didn't know how to begin. I encouraged him to speak freely. He then requested me to accompany him for a home-visit as he could not get the patient with him on his bicycle. He had travelled from a village that was more than twenty kilometres away.

My curiosity was piqued and to my own surprise, I agreed to go with him. When I reached his farm, he took me to his barn yard, straight to his bull, and said, 'Doctor Saheb, this is the patient!' I almost fainted in shock. He continued, 'Tomorrow there is a bull-fight in town where the judges will decide the category in which this bull will participate by examining his teeth. My bull lost one tooth in a practice session today and I request you to please fix it. Here is the tooth,' he said holding a big tooth wrapped in an old cloth in front of me.

I had, of course, never fixed a bull's tooth, but I was overwhelmed by the man's passion and decided to help him. Because of a large amount of saliva drooling from this patient's mouth, I had to use metres and metres of old saris instead of gauge pieces. With the help of the farmer and his family, I devised many innovative ways and was able to fix the bull's tooth.

A week later, the farmer came to my clinic with a box of sweets. The bull's tooth was doing fine and it had even won a shield in the bull-fight!

It has been more than thirty years now and I still receive a box of sweets from him, the owner of my unique patient, on the occasion of 'bail pola', a local festival of bulls!

Dr Vijay Parakh

Black Magic

After attending to patients the whole day, I was feeling sick and worn-out. The twilight was fast turning into darkness as I looked out of the window of my hostel in the All India Institute of Medical Sciences (AIIMS). It was a dull and boring evening and the very thought of plunging into assignments put me off. Our anatomy professor had given us a human skull to study over the weekend. I couldn't believe that I would have to spend my weekend with a skull for company!

Just then I got a call from my friend. 'Hey Ravi, come on dude, let's party! Kabir is treating us at Robbin's. Hurry up, before he changes his mind!'

Partying was a great way to de-stress; it was like a welcoming shower of rain on a patch of hot and thirsty land. I grabbed my bag and rushed out with my friends to catch the bus to Saket.

We boarded the bus and I was happy to find a vacant seat to rest my aching bones and muscles. The cool breeze stroked my face and within minutes I was fast asleep. When the bus braked I almost fell off my seat, and my friends had a good laugh at my expense. After that, in an effort to stay awake, I opened my bag and took out a book to read. But my fatigue got the better of me and I dozed off again.

'Aaah, ghost!' There was a loud shriek and the bus stopped abruptly. I was jolted out of my slumber by the screams of a young girl sitting in front of me. I looked around for my friends but could not see anyone. I looked out of the window and realised that I had left my stop behind. Wondering which ghost had the courage to come into a crowded bus, I stood up to probe the cause of the chaos and saw a human skull in the corridor of the bus.

'Oh ... that skull belongs to me. Don't be afraid!' I shouted to pacify the terrified crowd and walked through them to pick up my 'belongings'. Everyone was staring at me with wide open eyes.

'Who are you? Why do you carry such dangerous stuff with you? Are you a black magician?' There was a barrage of questions from all sides. Before I could explain, an old man yelled, 'I think he is a black magician. Let us take him to the police!'

'No, no, no ... I am not a black magician. I am a student of AIIMS, do not call the police. This is an assignment I had got from my professor. As the bus driver braked, this skull rolled out of my bag ...' I was trying desperately to convince the angry crowd but they refused to listen.

Just then, to my great relief, my friends came running towards the bus calling out to me. 'Ravi, we forgot to wake you up ... come on.'

'See ... these are my friends, they are with me. I am not a black magician!' I shouted nervously. We all showed our identity cards and the crowd calmed down, but they were still furious.

'Go away, you foolish doctor. None of us will ever come to get ourselves treated by a crazy boy like you!' shouted a lady and before the others could hurl more abuses at me, I ran out with my friends and didn't look back until I had reached Robbin's.

My friends had a hearty laugh when I narrated what had happened in the bus and I earned a new nickname that day — 'Dr Voodoo'!

Manish Chauhan

Mommy's 'Hungry Baby' Syndrome

As a paediatrician and a child specialist, my father obviously dealt primarily with children and their parents. Ever since I was a child, I was used to witnessing consultations: parents asking my father for a medical opinion and my father obliging them. It didn't matter where we were — at a party, aboard a train for a vacation, a social visit, or even at a Diwali get-together! Wherever we went, there was always someone who needed a medical opinion.

My father used to joke, 'There are two people who will always find a more than willing audience — one is a doctor and the other is an astrologer. Don't believe me? Board a train and say you are either of the two and in a second you will have ten people who want your advice.' He would always follow it up with, 'There's always a patient in every person and there's always an innate curiosity to know about the future.'

I had been a witness to this phenomenon. My father didn't try to be an astrologer but the mere mention of the 'Dr' before his name always brought an instant stream of people seeking his opinion. And as it turned out, some of the parents accompanying my father's 'patients' were quite interesting, because there's absolutely nothing in the world that can beat a zealous mother or father. Some of these consultations would always tickle my funny bone and they had the capacity to bring a smile on the most morose of faces. I remember one such incident, which later became a source of anecdotal storytelling for my dad, who always had a ready sense of humour at his disposal.

It was about six-thirty in the evening. My dad had returned from the Sir Sayajirao General Hospital, where he worked as a professor of paediatrics. Just as he finished his cup of tea, the door bell rang. One of our acquaintances was at the door; along with her was a woman with a one-and-a-half-year-old boy.

'This is my cousin's wife's sister,' said the aunty as a way of an introduction. I looked at the mother and the child. He was fair, his head was layered with soft, brown hair and a black dot rested at the corner of his forehead. As I looked at him, he flashed me a smile and then turned away to play with a ringlet of his mother's hair.

'Namaste,' said the mother.

'Namaste,' replied my father.

'I came to you for my boy, Sahib.'

'Yes? Tell me, is something the matter?'

'I am very worried. I have tried everything. You are my last hope.'

My father looked at the boy again and I could tell that he was a bit perplexed. 'What is the matter?'

'He doesn't eat.'

'No?' The boy, I forgot to mention, was cherubic in every sense of the term. He wasn't fat, he wasn't thin. In fact, he was perfect.

My father didn't even need the baby weighing scale to know that the baby boy in front of him weighed fine for his age.

'Hmm,' said my father. 'Tell me more.'

'See Sahib, try it right now. He will refuse to eat.' With that, the mother fished out a stainless steel tiffin box that contained porridge. As she scooped up a spoon of the porridge and held it towards her son, he turned his face away and pushed the spoon away.

'See what I mean? This is what he does, Sahib. Other children of his age eat so much. My son just refuses to eat. How will he grow up, Sahib?' The mother looked as if she could cry any moment.

'Do not worry. We will sort it out. Tell me something, what did you feed him last?'

'I fed him a mashed banana with milk.'

'That is very good,' said my father. 'You know what is nutritious for the child ... very good.'

The mother beamed.

'What else do you usually feed him?'

'Sahib, I make him porridge, sheera, I give him soft fruits, mashed potatoes and dal-rice. I never rely on tinned foods, I make everything myself.'

'You are such a well-informed mother; I always tell my patients that what you prepare in your kitchen is far better than what comes out of a tin. This is your first child, isn't it?'

'Yes, Sahib.' Her smile was like a crescent now. Her boy was gurgling.

'So tell me, this ripe banana and milk that you gave him. When was this?'

'Sahib, I fed him about twenty minutes ago. Was it twenty minutes, behen, or fifteen?' She looked at the older aunty for help.

'Fifteen minutes at the maximum, Tarla,' said the older aunty.

'Right,' said my father. 'Does your boy feel tired, or agitated?'

'No Sahib, he's full of energy.'

'Okay ... And how difficult is it to feed him?'

'Arrey Sahib, didn't you see just now? He refused to eat.'

'Right ... And when was it before this that he refused to eat. Can you tell me something about today?'

'Well, I fed him his breakfast in the morning and then he was playing. Just then, my neighbour came with a bowl of mashed potatoes and I tried to give him some and he refused. It happens almost every day.'

'You mean to say that he refuses food just after he's been fed or in other words, he's not hungry after being fed.'

The mother soaked it in for a moment. She didn't say anything.

My father gently prodded. 'I might be wrong here, but I am just asking. He's usually not willing to eat anything just a little while after he's been fed, right?'

'Yes Sahib.'

'Your child seems healthy. You are not wrong in your concerns. Most mothers believe that their children don't eat at all; especially first-time mothers. In fact, most mothers around the world would say something similar to what you are saying. They run around their children, chase them in order to feed them, they give them rewards — some mothers continue to do this even when their children are twenty or twenty-one!'

Everyone started laughing. The little boy was in my mother's arms by now. 'You see,' said my father, 'you are a good mother. You know what balanced meals are. Just feed him small meals at regular intervals but do not force-feed him, don't run after him and don't put in place a reward policy. He's growing well. It's just that, he's obviously not willing to eat just after he's been properly fed!'

When the mother and the elderly aunty left our house, my father turned to me and said, 'You have heard this before, haven't you?'

'Yes, Doctor Sahib, and I know what it is called — the "my son isn't hungry after he's fed syndrome"!' I burst out laughing as I said that and I could see that my mother was laughing too. But just when I thought we were done with it, she came up to my father and said, 'But even at this age, Prerna is such a poor eater. A pediatrician's daughter and yet so thin ...' I couldn't tell if she was jesting or serious!

Prerna Shah

Saviour

It was the month of August — not a great time to take a flight because the monsoon is at its peak in the north of India. It had been raining cats and dogs and the lightning and thunderstorms made it scary.

I was travelling from Ahmedabad to Jaipur. Because the flight was half empty, I was offered a seat in the business class at the normal fare, which I happily accepted. But minutes after take-off, all my joys of travelling in luxury vanished. The flight was rather bumpy because of bad weather. Every wobble of the aircraft made me uncomfortable and the passengers had started to panic. The pilot preferred to concentrate on flying rather than reassure passengers and all the crew members, including the air hostesses, seemed to have done a vanishing act.

My stomach churned at the sight of lightning and I was sure this would be my last flight. In the unstable aircraft, a passenger staggered towards the cockpit, and a few minutes later he was seen rushing back along with an air hostess. Soon there was an announcement. It was an air hostess asking if there was a doctor on board. The urgency in her voice grew and she had to repeat her request thrice before a passenger sitting on my left on the other side of the aisle raised his hand. The doctor was immediately escorted towards the sick passenger.

The flight finally landed safely and all of us heaved big sighs of relief.

The next evening I was at the Jaipur airport waiting to take my flight back to Ahmedabad. Suddenly, I spotted the doctor who had been my co-passenger the previous day. He looked surprised when I greeted him.

'Do we know each other?' he asked me. When I told him that I was the one sitting next to him on that memorable flight, he laughed heartily.

'Memorable … now! But, yesterday on that flight … I was so scared that I even forgot that I was a doctor! It was only the air hostess' repeated calls that jolted me out of my state of shock!'

He then remarked that it is very easy for doctors to start feeling like God, but every time that happens, God finds a way to shake them out of their castle in the sky and remind them that they are only human!

Sanjeev Trivedi

The Circus of Life

The date remains etched in my mind: 3rd December 1960. Ow! Oww! Owww! My father's wails grew louder and louder, alarming my mother and me. Nine years old, I stared at the man who was always in control, now clutching his stomach and rolling on his sides. The GP down the road had been summoned but perhaps it was the lateness of the hour that delayed his arrival. In the meantime neighbours had gathered at the window of our ground floor flat, and every wail brought in more people.

To tell the truth, it was more like roaring thunder than wails. My father's best friend (who was always there for the family — from babysitting me to being a mediator during emotional conflicts between my parents) was already on his way from the other side of the city. My mother was petrified and shivering as she saw the first streak of lightning and then the sound of thunder, heralding rain, which did not help matters.

The flat was small, but it had a large bedroom, and this room gradually began teeming with all sorts of people — well-wishers, pessimists, advisors, gossip-lovers and story-tellers who had tales of similar incidents. The stories were not at all encouraging. I would probably say that the room resembled an amphitheatre with the bed as the stadium. The prime seats (standing, of course) went to the immediate family and close friends, the next in line were the acquaintances who waited in the fringes.

To add to the confusion, my paternal grandparents were summoned as the situation turned from bad to worse. Sending for my grandparents should not have been an issue but the truth was, until some time ago, they had been estranged from my parents. As far as they were concerned, my mother was still persona non grata in their lives. But that, I am afraid, is another story.

So, when they arrived, my mother, who had no doubt dreaded this situation, seemed to fade away. Her tearful look reflected a combination of everything that was suddenly taking place in her life.

By this time, Dr Pal Chowdhury arrived with his black doctor's bag, and a frown on his face instead of the usual smile. I cannot recall how long it took him to come to a conclusion, but his diagnosis gave rise to a new crisis.

'He has acute appendicitis. It may burst any moment,' he declared.

I forget whether this announcement was made with conviction or not, but the next challenge was to get an ambulance. Though my father's job ensured he had access to Woodlands Nursing Home, probably the best nursing home then, for whatever reason, the ambulance had to be finally procured from the Calcutta Corporation. If you have never been in one of these, especially in the 1960s, I can only tell you that every bone in my body seemed to rattle during the ride in the ambulance.

Through all this I could only imagine my mother's condition, while my father's screams of agony were drowned by the clatter of all the equipment in the ambulance. By the time we reached the hospital it was past midnight.

Did our troubles end when we reached the nursing home? No. As my father lay in the ward while we waited downstairs, Dr Davies, one of the doctors on the panel of my father's company, drove in to the porch in his spotless white Ambassador. While he was rushing in, he asked his driver for his bag containing his instruments and was told, 'Sir, it is locked in the trunk. I have forgotten to bring the key, it is at home.'

All this I heard from my mother and my father's best friend later. Enraged, possibly cursing, the doctor looked all around for something with which to break the latch. Finding a big shovel that was possibly used to tend to the well-manicured lawn, and shooing away the driver who was grumbling about carrying out such a heinous act on the car, Dr Davies set himself to break the lock, in the process damaging his car. His fair face turned red as he brought the shovel down again and again till he finally succeeded in breaking open the boot, and in the process breaking away a good portion of it too, I believe. The driver sat holding his head in his hands, while the last glimpse we had of the doctor was of a disheveled person running inside with his bag.

Shortly afterwards, we were informed that the surgery had been successful; there had been minutes left for the appendix to burst, and my father was now asleep. Maybe we went back home or we slept in the waiting room; I don't seem to remember anything else of that night.

However, early next morning when we walked in almost on tenterhooks, remembering the agony and the trauma, a beaming face asked us, 'What's happening? What are you doing here and why are you looking at me like this?' The implication was that we should have been at home, fast asleep. We stared unbelievingly, not knowing whether to laugh or to cry. In a strangled voice, my father's mild-mannered best friend almost asked him to shut up.

Aditi Gaur

The Doctor Who Got Chicken Spots

My daughter Madhu had been unwell for a couple of days, when one morning she woke up covered in pink spots. She had so many you couldn't count them! One look and I knew what they were, for I was the eldest of eight children, and my weary mother had told me that for years we had taken turns to get infections and pass it on to our siblings — always one at a time. And we had all had chicken pox, one by one.

I rang the factory doctor. 'Madhu has chicken pox,' I said.

'Does she have fever?'

'About 101 degrees,' I said. 'But she's still eating okay.'

'Keep her in bed for a few days,' he said. 'And keep her away from old people. They can get really sick.'

He sighed, and added, 'It's an epidemic. I'm glad you didn't bring her to the clinic.'

The pharmacist sent Madhu pink pills for the fever and pink calamine lotion for the pink spots. After a couple of days she felt better, though very itchy. Her younger brother Tarun hovered around, extremely jealous that his sister had got chicken pox and left him out of it! He kept asking when he was going to get the chicken spots.

Living in the factory quarters was always a little lonely, but now it was worse. Our friends stayed away, and 'visited' on the phone. They offered all kinds of advice and herbal remedies, but we had to wait till all the scabs had fallen off before Madhu could go back to school and we could resume our social life. Even then, she had to visit the temple before she was considered completely cured!

Some days later Tarun woke us up very early to say he had chicken spots. I gazed at him fuzzily, not wishing to let go a pleasant dream about going to a party....

'You have chicken spots?' I said, groping for my glasses.

'Look!' he said, climbing on top of me so I could see the spot better. I peered at what was definitely a chicken pox spot.

'Oh, yes,' I said, 'you have a chicken spot.' I collapsed onto the pillow again, and tried to grab hold of my vanishing dream.

Tarun rushed away, shouting, 'I have a chicken spot! I have a chicken spot!'

'It's called chicken pox,' said Madhu sternly, and dabbed some calamine on the spot so that it wouldn't itch. We searched all over his skinny little body, but there was just this one rather large spot. My husband groaned when I told him.

'You mean we are back in quarantine again?' he groaned.

'I suppose so,' I said, and went to call the doctor.

Tarun was not content with just getting pink pills and calamine lotion; it was far too mundane, and he wanted some glory. The doctor visited the factory clinic three times a week, so after breakfast that day Tarun slipped out of the garden without informing anyone and went up to the clinic all by himself. There he sat surrounded by presumably sick factory workers, and made sure everybody knew he had a chicken 'spot'. By the time the doctor came he had sole rights on a long bench, and the workers were all clustered on the other side of the waiting room, as far as possible from the infectious boy.

Naturally the doctor called him in first, inspected the spot, and phoned me.

'Tarun has a chicken spot,' he said cheerfully.

'How do you know?' I asked.

'He's here at the clinic. It's definitely chicken spots.'

'You can't call it chicken pox any more, can you,' I said, laughing. 'We're all calling it chicken spots now. It's very catchy.'

He laughed too, and said, 'I'll send him back with a watchman.'

But I collected Tarun myself, because none of our watchmen wanted to escort him home. They were all afraid of getting chicken spots.

Madhu went back to school after her scabs fell off. Tarun got two more spots, one on his nose and another on his neck. He never had any fever nor did he fall sick. The chicken spots dried up, scabbed, and then left small pink marks. He went back to school gloating because he was the first in his class to get chicken spots.

About a week or ten days after Tarun's visit, the doctor himself became unwell. The next day when he looked in the mirror, he saw hundreds of spots on his body; he had caught chicken spots from somebody, perhaps from Tarun. He was so ill that had to stay in the hospital for two weeks, and convalesced at home for another month. I went to visit him after he came home, taking a bunch of flowers and some grapes, and of course Tarun was with me.

The doctor was covered in bright pink spots. Technically he was now non-infectious, since the all the scabs had fallen off, but he had lost weight and looked very weak. He was swathed in a thick shawl. His wife hovered near the door.

'I'm so sorry about your chicken spots,' I said, while Tarun looked in awe at the doctor who was supposed to never fall ill.

'You got a lot of chicken spots,' Tarun said. 'I only got three!'

'I only saw one on you,' said the doctor. 'It was a big one!'

'I got two more later,' said Tarun. 'Did I give you chicken spots?'

'Maybe,' said the doctor. There was a small silence. I reckoned we had pretty well exhausted the conversational possibilities of chicken spots, and prepared to leave. I handed the doctor the flowers and the grapes.

'I suppose you could call this the chicken spot prize,' he said, as his wife carried them into the house.

'It's because you got more chicken spots than anybody,' said Tarun.

The doctor grinned. 'I think I did get more spots, and do you know, now everybody calls it chicken spots,' he said. Then he looked very sternly at Tarun.

'The next time you get anything,' he said, 'you stay home and let your mother call me. Understand?'

'Is it because you might catch it?' Tarun asked, eyeing the splendid crop of chicken spots.

'Right,' said the doctor. 'Because I did catch it, and I know it was from you.'

'How did he know?' Tarun asked me later, as we walked back through the factory premises to our house.

'Know what?' I asked.

'That I gave him chicken spots?'

'Because he's a doctor, and doctors know everything,' I said. And that was that.

Jane Bhandari

The Lighter Moments of Medicine

There is no doubt that the study of medicine is a serious business. But that never prevented us medical students from looking for instances of humour wherever we could.

The first year in medical school is rightly called the anatomy year. Gray's *Anatomy Book* was our Bible and human bones our inseparable companions. College canteen tables would invariably sport a few of these bones most of the time, with some student or the other explaining their intricacies to his classmates. Human bones sharing the table with a plate of samosas may shock a stranger straying into the canteen, but for us medicos it was one of the most natural things to do.

We got on first-name basis with the cadavers and it was with heavy hearts that we dissected them, taking care to tell them what we planned to do. We, of course, knew that it made no difference to the cadavers, but it helped us to revise and remember!

More than anything else, we learnt in the anatomy laboratory the art of holding our breath for long durations (if possible, we would have totally avoided breathing to escape the smell), and not to blink when the formalin fumes were all pervading.

With this training, we could have even faced tear gas shells successfully.

In the second year, we started our clinical posting which, among other things, included taking down a history of the patient's complaints. The patient arrives in the OPD (out patients' department) with all the symptoms of a damaged liver, but would never admit what led to it. Here is where we used psychological tactics to our advantage. We had to prod him enough to get to the truth. It went along these lines:

'Do you drink?'

'No, absolutely not.'

'Social drinking has become very common nowadays. You can't help it once in a while if the occasion calls for it,' I say casually.

'Yes, but that is only very occasionally.'

I follow the lead. 'Meeting friends on weekends has to be celebrated with a drop of liquor.'

'You are right, weekends go that way.'

I move on smoothly. 'Tension at the workplace during the day makes one wish for a drink in the evenings to settle the nerves.'

'You are very understanding. I must admit that tension makes me have a glass in the evenings.'

We are nearing the truth. Oozing sympathy, I add, 'I am sure sometimes in the mornings also, before going to work.'

He starts to become a bit cautious. 'Yes, but not very often.' Thus I get the confession and, smiling to myself, I record on the case paper 'habitual drinker'.

Once, we were sitting in the gallery of the OT (operation theatre) to watch the seniors operate, and while they went about the business of locating a kidney stone, to our great surprise, they also started humming in chorus 'Dhoondo dhoondo re sajana dhoondo ....!' That scene decided it for me. I chose my (future) post-graduation branch then and there — if surgery is all song and dance as it appeared to be, that was where I would be going.

However, it was much later, after I qualified as a surgeon, that I learnt with experience that the poor guys had not been having a lark, but trying to hide their nervousness and contain their tension.

A patient coming out of anaesthesia is another story; all inhibitions go awry and, at times, they end up saying things they would never do otherwise. Hallucination is a very common condition. Once a woman told me confidentially that she was getting ready to fly! I just prayed that she may also decide to land gently when the anaesthesia effects wore off!

During the period of internship, the students are forever on their toes when they are posted to various departments on rotation. An overworked friend of mine posted to the gynaecology department told me that she had just sent a petition to god to suspend the reproduction business for some time.

'For how long?' I asked.

'Well, till my gynaecology posting gets over,' she said.

Thus, though it was mostly 'all work' for us, we saw to it that we extracted some fun out of such situations so that we did not get affected by the pain and anxiety around. I would not trade those years of mine at the medical college for anything.

Everything in life has a lighter side. We only have to go looking for it!

Ramya Nisal

8

JUST DOING THEIR JOB

A doctor must work eighteen hours a day and seven days a week. If you cannot console yourself to this, get out of the profession.

—Martin H. Fischer

A Lifetime of Living

Every morning my husband and I go to the club for a walk. We often meet this gentleman there, in his sixties, who smiles and greets us. 'Don't you remember that we had dinner at his place on Janmashtami, many years ago?' said my husband one day when he realised I was trying to figure out where I'd met the old man.

Then I remembered the incident ... the children were very young then and liked going to the Law Garden every Saturday evening, where they would enjoy taking horse rides and sitting on the merry-go-round. Before returning home, we would buy balloons and ice-creams for them. Our Saturday evenings were something that we all looked forward to after a long, hard week.

That particular Saturday evening, the children and I were all dressed and ready to leave for our outing. My husband was just about to lock the door of the house when the phone rang. He went inside to pick it up and then rushed out to inform us that he couldn't join us as he had to leave immediately to attend an emergency call.

'Why can't you come with us, Daddy? You never come anywhere with us,' the children cried.

Seeing their distress, I told my husband, 'Why don't you come with us first? We can go for just half an hour. You can see the patient a little later.'

But my husband insisted that he had to go that very minute and urged us all to go ahead without him. I, too, was upset and kept on insisting that before going to his patient, he must join us. However, my husband went off to see the patient leaving us there on the doorstep of the house. I stomped back inside with the howling children in tow, and we ended up just watching TV that evening.

The next day, my husband told me that the patient was doing well, thanks to the timely medical action. Some days later, the patient's wife came to our house to invite us all for dinner on Janmashtami. I remember the party very well and the house, which was a particularly beautiful one. It had a long driveway and a garden with a water body. The house had big glass doors, lovely art hung on the walls and there were statues in every nook and corner. The house was overflowing with friends and relatives, all laughing and joking, while children played all over the place.

We lost contact with the family for more than twenty years until I met the old man recently. He must be in his late sixties or early seventies now and looks content with his life. Every time I see him, I think about that Saturday evening long ago. What was just a spoiled evening for me has meant a lifetime of living for him with his wife, children and friends.

Bhagyashree Sowani

Communicate

I was three years old when I first experienced the importance of doctor-patient communication and how it could build trust and expedite the healing process.

I had been diagnosed with gastroenteritis by the paediatrician and he told my mother that it was critical to keep me hydrated.

'Plenty of oral fluids,' he exhorted.

His cardinal mistake was that he failed to communicate this advice to me, the patient. My sister, on the other hand, who was fifteen months older than me, explained the advice in her own words to me.

'Don't drink anything,' she cautioned, wise from personal experience. 'You'll vomit if you do.'

Since she was my god-cum-doctor-cum-role model, I kept my mouth stubbornly shut while my mother tried to make me sip fluids. Fortunately for me, the gastroenteritis was self-limiting and I did not shrivel up and die!

When I grew up, I went on to train to be a doctor. Influenced as I was by early childhood experiences, I have always strived to use the power of communication to good effect. Despite the best intentions in the world, sometimes the results are totally unexpected.

I am now an eye specialist in a government hospital. Once, early in my career, I spent precious minutes in a hectic OPD explaining to a patient that the drops were to be used three times a day for a week. The patient ruminated while I mentally tapped my fingers, itching to call in the next patient.

Finally, she looked at me and said in all innocence, 'Do I take them with meals or on empty stomach?'

I all but gasped, realising that it is not enough to just communicate, you must communicate right! And that means that the patient must comprehend what you mean. It was a lesson for me; I had taken it for granted but the patient didn't know the difference between eye drops and oral drops!

Now I always say, 'Please use these drops in your eyes!'

Then there is the problem of who is the best person to talk to when the patient is a child. I learnt this the hard way; try as I might I could not convince a mother to stop using a shared kajal stick in her baby's eyes. Every visit would find the baby's eyes outlined in black. Finally, after listening uncomfortably to my harangue on the evils of sharing kajal sticks, the mother blurted out, 'My mother-in-law insists. She says my son will have small, beady eyes if I don't put kajal everyday.'

I realised that I had been flogging the wrong horse. In a moment I had elicited a promise that the mother-in-law would accompany them on the next visit. It took some doing, but I have since learnt the art of convincing fond grandmothers to abandon practices that might cause more harm than good!

Another predicament I have is when I offer two or more treatment options as a part of 'informed consent'. The patient has to choose one based on the information I provide. Decisions are guided by comparative cost, convenience, duration of follow up, and many other things. After talking at length, and having assured myself that the patient understands, I ask for their choice. I am often frustrated by the response I get.

'Doctor Sahib,' my informed patient is prone to say. 'You know best. You decide ...'

Just another day at the office!

I have been at it for a quarter century now; it is exhausting, demanding, challenging, stressful, but never, ever have I found it to be boring.

Dr Upreet Dhaliwal

From the Wallet

My neighbour once told me a story about a man who was charged for a by-pass surgery that he never had. He was taken to the OT and brought out with a scar, but years later, it was discovered that nothing had been done. They do it for money, she confidently stated. Even newspapers carry stories of patients duped by 'nursing homes' in the name of surgeries and hours later find a kidney missing ... which surfaces by chance after a couple of years of abdominal pain. Neither of the above surgeries can be done by a single doctor, a highly qualified and skilled team is required.

On the other hand, I have many stories of how doctors really do play angels, if not god, ever so often. Once, when I was in the charity department, I remember two young registrars who'd travelled with a precious cerebral fluid sample all the way from beyond Thane. They'd personally taken the trouble lest someone lose or drop it. They were given partial concession, the rest they had to pay. They didn't have that much money, so they messaged a friend to get the rest while they waited. Such dedication to an anonymous patient! Money certainly wasn't motivating them to do this.

My spine surgeon, after my three miserable episodes of agonising back pain, personally bent, stretched and twisted to show me how I should do the correct exercises. Not once, but several times, so that I got it right and did it right. He needn't have taken the trouble, but he did. He, like many others, doesn't charge 'people who make a difference to the society'. A lot of time, effort and skill are given for free.

When I hear people say 'all doctors are greedy', I wonder, will the airlines pay for a desperate passenger who wants to secure a seat to attend his interview? Medical professionals deal with desperate people. A passenger flying for a job interview is equally desperate. So we can't jump to conclusions casually.

I remember an out-station patient who had to wear a metal collar post neurosurgery. The surgeon paid the rent for that collar, and made sure the patient wore it for a couple of months. Later an acquaintance brought it back after its use was over. A year later, the surgeon made a trip to the patient's village to see how he was doing. Still think all doctors are greedy?

Dr A, a gentle soul, was forever digging into her purse to pay for someone's medicines. I had to warn her that people were taking her for granted but she wouldn't listen; instead she would say 'I've more than enough, these people are in trouble, let it be if once in a while someone does take advantage.'

In the hospital where I worked, sometimes donors would come and ask me which patient needed help. I was particular that the money should be wisely used. I'd check with the doctors whose bill was likely to shoot up and more importantly, whether the patient's outcome was likely to be good. If the prognosis was poor, if the patient was likely to die, I wouldn't spend the donor's money on him, but search for a salvageable case.

Once, a sixteen-year-old girl in the ICU had a huge outstanding bill. Her parents were middle-class and not in a position to raise the funds, nor were they eligible for any concession. So I checked with the doctor whether she'd 'make it'. He was annoyed and said that he would do everything to see that girl go back home, cured and happy; till then he would personally see that she got treatment under him. And how dare I ask such a question? If she was admitted under him, money or not, he'd continue to treat her, okay? Such is the passion and commitment doctors display, and mind you, this happened in a private hospital.

The samples given by pharmaceutical companies have saved many lives, and brought comfort to many patients. That's not all, I know of a doctor who paid his patient's son's fees too. It was not enough to treat him medically; the holistic treatment meant the patient's mind had to be at ease and his future secure.

So now, whenever I hear rumours about such-and-such patient's experience of having a surgery not done yet paid for, or unnecessary surgeries recommended, I ask for details. Quite often, the sources are nameless or likely a figment of someone's imagination.

Sheela Jaywant

Humility: The Hallmark of Greatness

My ulcer has been my constant companion for the past fifteen years. Ever since it got lodged in my stomach, no medication seemed effective against it. Under the onslaught of a variety of pills and concoctions, it would stay quiet for a while, but after a few days the ulcer would rear its ugly head again. A major chunk of my husband's salary was spent in buying medicines and this was driving a wedge in our saving plans. Meanwhile the strict diet was making me irritable and difficult to live with — imagine a foodie being stuck with boiled vegetables and mashed fruits all day long. I was feeling absolutely wretched about the whole thing, as a decade and a half of such frugal diet and medication had not yielded any results.

Naturally, when my uncle suggested I meet a gastroenterologist my first response was 'no'. I was tired of taking chances with a myriad of doctors and coming back disappointed. But he somehow convinced me and I reluctantly asked him the doctor's name.

'Dr K.R. Palaniswamy, a senior consultant gastroenterologist at Apollo, Chennai. Have you heard of him?' asked my uncle feigning innocence.

Of course, I had heard of him. He was one of the best in his field. How could I even afford his fee? There would be a huge dent in my coffers if I went to him. But my uncle was very stubborn and he nearly dragged me to Dr Palaniswamy. When my turn came, he said in jest, 'I shall wait here outside the room to catch you lest you decide to run away.'

His humourous taunt, however, did nothing to ease the knots in my stomach. I could feel my ulcer acting up again as my head buzzed with doubts. What if he prescribes costly medicines? What if he brushes aside my questions? What if ....? I did not have to think about the third misgiving because I had a glimpse of the doctor and he was nothing like I had imagined. This kindly man with a warm smile surely could not be the 'can't-spare-more-than-a-minute' haughty medico that I had imagined.

'Please come.' His pleasant voice jolted me out of my thoughts. I was armed with my medical files and got ready to explain my illness in detail but he just glanced at the files and put them aside.

'Okay, Ma, I will ask you a question and I want an honest answer. Have there been any recurrent problems in the family? I assure you whatever you say will never leave this room.'

One look at him and I knew he would keep his word. He was the kind of brotherly figure with whom one would immediately feel at ease. I found myself pouring out painful details that I had never shared with anyone.

For the past fifteen years, my family had been going through a lot of ups and downs. It started when my husband lost his job and then a spate of financial losses, bereavements, and familial estrangements had taken their toll. Now my husband had a steady job, but the constant tension about the unforeseeable future had left me an emotional wreck.

When I paused for breath, shaken by the recollection of the painful events, he passed me a glass of water and asked me to relax. Then he gently said, 'Most stomach ulcers have their roots in, and are aggravated by emotional triggers. If we have no personal problems we may be able to eradicate ulcers completely. Unfortunately, problems will always be there. If we want our body to be fit we have to face the problems and cope with them positively. Brooding or worrying about them will only worsen the situation.

'I will prescribe some tablets for you and put you on a suitable diet, but the main effort has to come from within you. You have to control your emotions and not the other way round. Do we have a deal?'

It was his gentle demeanour, his soft probing into my disturbed mental state and his confidence in helping me to look at life a little more positively, that did the trick. I was half relieved of my mental pressures when I divulged the pain I had within and the rest came gradually with the sense of self-worth he imparted to me.

When he quoted his fee, it was so nominal I could not believe it. Even the medicines cost much less than the ones I had been taking till then. With the new drugs, controlled diet (which included a lot of my favourite items) and positive thinking, I have kept the ulcer at bay for the past five years.

Of course, the regular visits to the doctor have been the main catalyst in my progress. In the past five years, Dr Palaniswamy has gone from strength to strength, yet for me and all his patients, he has remained the same old, affable Palani Anna. His holistic approach and patience have cured many a patient as much as his diagnosis has.

Kalaivani Asokan

India Has It

Mother emotionally blackmailed me into getting a yearly health check-up done when I was visiting her this time. She pulled me out of the house, where I was busy cleaning — my passion. To our surprise, we met a cheerful doctor with out-of-the-box thinking.

'Your haemoglobin count is far too low,' the doctor announced, after reading my reports.

'Yes, but all the other tests are fine, right?' I defended my body's self-esteem.

'Well, what is the use of a perfect system that has no energy to function?'

'Well, Doc, with due respect, during the last few days, I have washed eight curtains by hand, not in the machine. I swabbed the floor of the apartment, washed a huge carpet and washed the terrace. Now, if not with energy then God must have come to help out, right?" I hoped the doctor got the picture.

'Well, even the labourers who work on construction sites do a lot of physical work. With low iron count, they suddenly collapse. You want to collapse too?'

'No. Okay, Doc, tell me which iron pills do I need to swallow.'

'Iron pills are quite useless. You will have to change your diet.'

'Oh,' I was flabbergasted.

'The only answer is nutrition.'

'You mean, you are not going to prescribe any pills?'

'Nope.'

'Okay, tell me Doc, what should I eat?'

'All this is for a day, and every single day.' Thus saying he gave me a list of nutritious food, and then said, 'In addition to these, don't keep yourself hungry for long. Keep snacks ready with you at all times. For one month don't count calories, and after that, test your blood count again. If you have followed this diet to the T, and your count does not increase, mera naam bhi Doctor nahin.'

'Can I say something, Doc? This is very surprising, because doctors rarely talk about nutrition.'

'If they did, who would come to them? They also have to look after their stomachs, isn't it?' joked the doctor.

'I am so glad to meet a doctor without a stomach, Doc. Thank you!'

Anna Hazare, India has it!

Manjushree Abhinav

Pain in the Neck

Sometimes ailments that evade diagnosis cause more worry than the deadliest of diseases. I went through such a phase when I was in my early thirties. That was nearly four decades ago, but the pain and agony I suffered are still fresh in my mind. I shudder to think what would have happened if I had not met Dr P.C. Sen.

The year was 1976. After a hectic working day, I was relaxing at home with a steaming cup of tea when I suddenly felt an excruciating crick in my neck. Applying a balm reduced the intensity, but the next day the pain was back. My head and neck felt as if they would explode. Maybe the year-end work pressure was getting to me, I thought, and decided to give my aching body a rest. I called in sick at the office and relaxed with painkillers and coffee, but at the end of the day the ache only worsened. Self-diagnosis had obviously been way off target.

I met my family doctor who said it might be the preliminary stages of spondylitis and prescribed some pills for pain relief, but to no avail. The stubborn cramp remained as strong as ever. Next, on the recommendation of colleagues, I consulted Ayurveda experts who gave me an herbal paste to be applied to the affected area. Again the respite was temporary. Each time the pain returned, it increased in power while my energy to face it diminished rapidly.

I took long leave and decided to stay at home till the menace went away. It was probably a wrong move because now the Devil had a free run of my idle mind to set up his workshop. Thoughts of stroke, paralysis' and other critical illnesses crowded my brain and that increased my tension.

By now the pain had taken over my life completely. My blood pressure shot up to alarming levels. I put on weight due to my sedentary lifestyle. And worse, I was dependant on my wife for small things like getting up from bed, walking to the rest room, sitting in a chair, etc. She had to support my neck and help me up from a sleeping position to a standing one; she had to hold my hand and take me here and there; when the discomfort became unbearable (which was almost always) she had to even feed me.

Meanwhile my trysts with alternate medication continued as I shifted from homoeopathy to Siddha to Reiki, but all in vain.

I was on the verge of depression when my colleague called me and asked me to consult a Dr P.C. Sen putting me in a dilemma. I was desperate to try anything that would cure my condition, but paradoxically I was ready to give up on all medical advice out of frustration. Finally, desperation won over frustration and I took an appointment to visit Dr Sen's clinic the following day. I tried to quell the anticipation that I felt each time I tried a new path because the end result usually turned out to be a damp squib.

One look at me, a few questions, a routine examination of the neck and he gave his verdict: neck osteoarthritis. His diagnosis was over in five minutes flat. He gave me a few tablets to take and asked me to come back in a week's time.

I came away feeling conned out of my money. How could he have reached a conclusion about my illness in such a short time without asking me to take X-rays, blood tests and the works? I was tempted not to have the tablets but something made me.

The miracle started as early as the next day. Just one pill and my pain was almost gone. After a week, I was a new man. It was as if the ache had never been there. I rushed to the doctor's clinic with a big box of sweets and a heart full of gratitude.

The bond, thus established, remained strong for twenty years till he retired from practice due to old age. Now his soul rests in heaven, but he is alive in the thoughts of countless patients like me, to whom he gave a new lease of life.

Ravindranath Sharma

The ICU

I was one of the top honchos in an organisation that specialised in managing events, and holding medical conferences was one of them. My work entailed not only back-end work but also marketing and having face-to-face meetings with CEOs, specialist medicos, etc.

One of the events we were pitching for required a visit to a surgeon who was in charge of the ICU (intensive care unit) of a local hospital. Since she was extremely busy, the only place we could visit her was the ICU. So we went there to meet her; my boss and I.

The ICU is an enervating place; patients there are in the crucial situation hovering between life and death. All around us were grieving and anxious relatives. Some tried to take comfort from each other, encouraging them to hold on and pray. We tried to shut ourselves from the pain and the mental anguish.

It seemed impossible!

We looked at doctors and interns who seemed impervious to the anguish of the relatives and calmly went about their jobs, calling for a nurse here, a specialist there, accompanying a patient on a trolley or wheeling out a dead body.

The more time we spent in the ICU, the more we found ourselves able to disconnect from the reality around us, to tune out the crying, to ignore the tears.

'This is how they do it,' I thought to myself, 'this is how doctors and surgeons are able to handle grief. They just tune out. It's just another statistic to them.'

And then in walked the nephrologist with whom we were coordinating for a medical conference. He didn't notice us at first and went on his rounds, moving from bed to bed to check on his patients. When he was diagonally opposite us across the large room, he spotted us.

Without hesitation, he handed his clipboard to an intern and almost ran across to us.

'Is everything okay?' he asked anxiously. 'Do you have someone here in the ICU?'

I was stunned!

Here was someone we had met on business, with whom we had dealt on financials and practicalities and sponsors and other mundane issues. Here he was, in the ICU where specialists and even interns apparently steel themselves to the harsh realities in order to be able to sleep at night. And here he was in front of us, distressed that one of us might have a relative in the ICU. The concern in his stance, voice and face was unmistakably genuine.

In a scarce couple of hours, I was able to tune out the anguish. In the midst of decades of practice in the ICU, he was able to retain his concern.

Deepak Morris

9

DEALING WITH TRAGEDY

Even hundredfold grief is divisible by love.
—Terri Guillemets

Circa 1988

A couple, my patients for over eight years, had a second baby girl when their elder one was six years old. The newborn Neha turned out to be a physically challenged child. The parents were well educated and without batting an eyelid, got down to raising the baby.

The mother was a housewife and spent all her time either looking after the child or gathering information about what was being done around the world for similarly challenged kids. The father was a member of the flying crew in one of the international airlines and his shopping list consisted of books and gadgets to aid his child's therapy.

All was well till the child turned five, when one day she got her first seizure and had to be hospitalised. The parents were shattered; things were difficult as such and now this ever-hanging sword — would she have another seizure?

Things took a turn for the worse. Neha's convulsions came with increasing frequency; she was in and out of hospitals. Although it was a big drain financially, the parents never ever thought of going to second-grade hospitals or ever doubted the prognosis. They relentlessly pursued Neha's treatment always hoping for a miracle.

One day in 1998, after Neha had just turned ten, she went into status epilepticus (a condition in which repeated epileptic seizures occur without the patient gaining consciousness in between) and had to be hospitalised in the ICU of one of the best hospitals of Mumbai. Four days of recurrent seizures left Neha brain dead.

As her family physician, it was up to me to break the news to her parents. In the lobby outside the ICU, I took them to a corner and explained Neha's condition and the futility of continuing treatment. They must have realised that it was the end of the road, but when asked to sign documents authorising the hospital authorities to stop treatment, Asha, Neha's mother, screamed out: 'How can you, Doctor? How can you even suggest such a thing? You know how much we have tried to keep her happy?'

Keeping a brave face, I again explained to Asha the futility of continuing treatment and the torture Neha must be going through. Asha angrily turned to me and asked, 'Doctor, would you talk like this if she was your own daughter?' And with that she burst out crying.

All my communication skills had not prepared me for this question. Completely trusting the veracity of what I had suggested, I looked into Asha's eyes and said without blinking, 'If she was my daughter, I would have done so forty-eight hours earlier. As she was not, I waited for these extra two days.'

Something must have touched Asha — either my words or the way they were said, and she signed the documents.

Now they stay in New Zealand but they never forget to send me a card every year on the same date, thanking me for making the agony bearable.

Dr Chandramohan Asrani

Lady Saviour

It was a Wednesday, I remember, because we had an activity class in school. I hated the swimming sessions, but that day I forgot all about it and was very excited, as I knew I was going to hear the most wonderful news when I got back home.

My mother had gone to visit a doctor. I really wished that she would bring good news of a little baby brother. I knew God would grant me my wish, and my eyes were constantly on the clock waiting for her to come back.

I was too restless and excited to watch the Disney show and I didn't even go for my dance classes. How could I be away when Mom came home with the wonderful news?

Finally the doorbell rang, and I ran to open the door, only to see my mother's gloomy face. I had never seen her so unhappy; her eyes were red and her hands were trembling. Even Dad's face reflected tension and sadness.

'Mom … it doesn't matter if I am not getting a baby brother. Please don't get upset. I love you …we all love you!' I said.

Later I was so confused when she pulled me into her arms. I had never seen her cry so loudly before.

Months passed by after this incident. I got busy with my school assignments and other activities. I promised God that I would share my building blocks and bicycle with my brother ... if only I could have him soon. I kept my fingers crossed!

Gradually, I observed many changes in my Mom. Her face grew pale, her hair was falling and her eyebrows had almost disappeared. Something was wrong but nobody would tell me anything.

I decided to find out the truth. I knew Mom went to the nearby hospital to meet the doctor so I went straight to meet her after school (after completing my swimming lessons).

The 'gyaneclist' was so young. I thought she would be an old lady with a grumpy face, but she was rather beautiful with a sweet voice. But I still don't know why she broke into tears when she saw me.

'What happened to Mom? Every time she visits you, she comes back home in a bad mood. What do you tell her?'

'Nothing at all sweetheart ... your Mom is fine. She will recover in a few days.'

'I don't want a baby brother if it causes so much trouble to my Mom, okay?'

'Hmmm ... okay. I will try my best to reduce her troubles. Now smile!'

Back home I heard Granny yelling at Mom, 'How could you hide this from me? I had told you to do the rituals at Trimbakeshwar. It was written in your horoscope ... danger to health at thirty ... but I never imagined it would be cancer!'

Cancer? I had heard about it on TV ... even the newspapers had written about it. The next door aunty had once said that it is a 'killer disease'. Was my Mom dying? I went running back to the hospital.

'Doctor aunty … my Granny says Mom has cancer ….' I couldn't speak. The tears flowed right into my mouth and stopped my words.

'Not at all darling … there is nothing wrong with your mother … she's fine!'

'I know she isn't! Save my mother please!' I did not taste the chocolates that she gave me. All I wanted to know was about cancer and the horrible effects it would have on Mom.

I didn't see Mom for months. Even though Doctor aunty called home a few times, Mom never spoke to me. Perhaps she did not want me to hear her sad voice.

In January, Mom came back home! Everything seemed perfect. All that I missed was the softness of her chest when I hugged her. They had removed it; my mother had survived breast cancer.

I know it was Doctor aunty who saved Mom. She proved Granny wrong.

Whatever you call her, gyaneclist or doctor, she is my God because she kept her word to me. She is the one who granted my wish. Even though I am not going to have a baby brother, it doesn't bother me now. I have my Mom!

My Doctor aunty has solutions to every problem and I will be a saviour like her one day. I will be a doctor … perhaps a … gynaecologist … one day!

Reshmi Kurup

One Last Visit

Like most people, I did not like visiting hospitals as the sight of patients and the pain and suffering disturbed me. But ironically, I became a regular visitor to a particular hospital after my dad was diagnosed with cancer at an advanced stage.

Those were the most painful days of my life. Dad was hospitalised for three weeks before he passed away. After that I developed a loathing for the hospital from where Dad couldn't come back home, and for the doctor who had prescribed the chemotherapy. I felt it was because of that treatment that Dad suffered multiple organ failure which eventually took him away from us.

I do not know how rational my grudges were, but nevertheless I preserved them. I promised never to visit that hospital again. But I could not hold on to my pledge for long as I needed to get Dad's death certificate from the hospital.

'This will be my last visit,' I thought to myself as soon as I had taken the death certificate from the reception. I was anxious to get out of the hospital premises. But on my way out, on an impulse, I turned around and walked towards the room where Dad had stayed during the course of his treatment.

I stood outside the door of that room, visualising Dad sleeping on the bed and me sitting next to him. As I recollected the scene, tears poured down my cheeks; I just could not control myself. Just as I was wiping my tears, I felt a hand on my shoulders. I looked back, only to discover the same doctor, whom I detested, smiling at me. I smiled back half-heartedly.

Then he told me something really amazing that shook me. He said, 'When I was in high school, I too lost my father to cancer in this hospital. Within a few months after he passed away, I decided to study medicine and ultimately serve people here as an oncologist.'

I was too stunned to speak and left the hospital with a gamut of thoughts racing in my mind. The doctor and I both had been through the same pain, we had both lost our fathers in the same hospital and to the same terminal illness, but we had reacted so differently. While I decided to avoid the place of my anguish forever and allowed hatred to consume me, he channelised the intensity of his emotions by making the hospital his work place and serving cancer patients as a doctor.

Saurabh Paul

The Escape

'Doctor, I want to die,' my mother told the doctor just as he was starting her dialysis session. A nurse was holding her arm down as he inserted a big needle into an already swollen vein in her left forearm. The catheter implanted in her left wrist was whirring unusually fast. I saw the doctor's face turn pale; Doc had made this his battle too.

'This is not done Mrs Nayak…' he said. 'You have to be brave and give me time.' It was more of an order than a request. He was not ready to give up on her. Behind that bespectacled, confident face, I noticed his eyes grow dim with worry. It was a year since my mother had been diagnosed with acute renal failure.

'I can see it. Death is approaching me!' my mother insisted. I just couldn't wait by her side, for its arrival! I felt my legs break into a trot and my heart throb with intense pain as I ran out of the hospital. A nerve in my head was beating like a thousand hammers as I sprinted down, tears streaming down my cheeks. I did not care about the onlookers; I was trying to escape.

During my mother's regular dialysis sessions at the hospital, Doc would do everything to try and ease her pain. He was always concerned about her and did all he could. Despite the queue outside his office, he would take time out to come and chat with her, assuring her of a new life after a kidney transplant. Doc helped build my mother's hopes and strengthened her will to endure the excruciatingly painful dialysis sessions. My mother trusted him so much that she was totally dependent on him and never allowed anybody other than him to insert the needles connected to the dialyzer.

I travelled farther away from the hospital in hope that this was a nightmare that would end as soon as I reached home. I was dreaming of going back home where my mum would be waiting at the window for me. My loving mother would instantly leave all her work and attend to my needs, bringing a cool glass of water at my arrival. I was speeding towards the yummy food she kept piping hot and ready for me. I was trying to escape into my happy past, away from this horrible present.

But of course everything had truly changed forever. I got home and bawled like a baby.

Suddenly my cell phone began to vibrate. It was Doc calling. My feeble greeting was received with a reprimand: 'Come back to the hospital right away!' I could sense great tension in his voice. What was wrong? I cursed myself for being such a coward and headed back.

Like a close relative would, Doc was there, fretting over Mum's deteriorating condition. She had gone into a coma, but he was the only other person, other than my father and me, who was not ready to accept that my mother had finally succumbed to acute renal failure. He was completely positive that she would wake from the coma, soon. 'Well ... and smiling, you'll see!' Doc said patting me kindly. His touch told me he understood my plight and gave me the much needed sense of security. Through the next few days, we saw an increasing number of doctors come visiting. Doc had harnessed all possible help from the medical fraternity to revive my mother.

It's easy to hit the Esc key. One click and you can free yourself from an error. In the real world, it's also very easy to be an escapist, turning numb to emotions and other's pain. Doc needn't have wasted his precious days for this patient, my mother, one amongst the many others he was taking care of. Like I had run away to my empty house, he could have escaped too but as promised he never gave up hope. And on the ninth day, they successfully brought my mother back to me, alive and well, as promised.

Doc had helped her escape death. I buried my face in her lap and cried. This doctor had given me what I had prayed for ... some more time with my mother. Some more time to tell her how much I loved her, some more time to show her what the Doc exemplified — 'Where there is a will, there is a way', and time to mentally prepare myself for the worst.

They may talk of unethical malpractices by doctors in India but I think some conscientious and brave doctors still exist, who readily embrace the emotional baggage their job sometimes entails. I was fortunate enough to meet one such doctor who never tried to escape his responsibilities, one who still felt human emotions in this extremely calculative, materialistic world.

Vibhuti Bhandarkar

The God Complex

Not many people get the chance to save someone's life, let alone save a lot of lives on a regular basis the way we doctors do. When you bring someone back from the dead, it's an unimaginable feeling of pride, elation and yes, over time, you develop a 'god complex'.

The following incident took place during my post-graduation days.

I knew it was going to be a long day the first time I came across Vikas. He was being shifted out of the operation theatre into the ICU directly. The previous night he'd been a victim of a road accident. A hit-and-run case, just another twenty-year-old crossing the road on his way back to his hostel.

The kid was a mess. His head was clean-shaven and disfigured, a part of his skull having been placed in his thigh to prevent further pressure to his damaged brain. His spleen, torn during the accident, had been removed. He'd lost more than half his blood in those six hours. The neurosurgeon who operated on him gave him no chance of survival. He was comatose and in shock, requiring a ventilator, a dozen blood transfusions and endless drugs to keep him alive.

Over the next nine days, we got to know his father well as he stayed by his son's side. His mother was in another hospital in their home town, admitted with shock after hearing the news. His father got to meet his friends and professors. He also got to meet his son's girlfriend for the first time. He accepted her as she was as much a part of Vikas's life as he was. When the specialists weren't looking in on him, the residents were monitoring him in shifts twenty-four hours a day even as nurses bathed, fed, cleaned and shaved him.

On the seventh day, the miracle began. The kid no one had any hopes for was weaned off all cardio-supportive drugs. His heart was supporting his body now all by itself.

On the eleventh day, this kid with his skull in his thigh opened his eyes. It was as if he had been asleep all along. He had minimal control over his left limbs, a consequence of the accident. He could mouth words, but not speak them because of the tracheostomy which had been done in view of the prolonged respiratory support.

On the twelfth day, he developed a lung infection. We helped him overcome it in just four days. Aggressive management was the key phrase in all our minds. This kid with the misshapen head was working overtime to stay alive. We knew he had it in him to do it. He'd been through the darkness, and he just needed us to get him past the last hailstorms and into the light. Vikas was the conversation starter in many a doc's greeting in those days.

By the fourteenth day, he had enough power to lift his right hand and scratch his head — a casual gesture for you and me, but that movement made our day and we doctors laughed with pride that evening over coffee.

By the seventeenth day, Vikas was bored of his walkman. You would be too, if you had to listen to it during all your waking hours. He was too weak still to stay awake for long periods, but we needed to keep him stimulated during those few hours that he was awake, be it 3 a.m. or 5 p.m. A doctor's laptop was procured, and we filled him up on what was going on in the world. His girlfriend told us his favourite actresses and we got him those movies. His girlfriend held his hand throughout whenever he was awake in a way that only a person who loves you can. His dad was there through it all, willing his son to 'become the miracle'.

By the nineteenth day, we removed his ventilator support. Vikas's lungs, heart and brain were now strong enough to take him through. His body would pull through with adequate nourishment. The neurosurgeon who operated on him told him he had done the impossible. We celebrated like kings after a victorious siege that night.

On the twenty-second day, we took Vikas out of the ICU for an hour. We pushed his bed around the hospital, three doctors in attendance. We filled him in on the raunchy jokes we had in our repertoire and rejoiced in his half smile.

On the twenty-fifth day, at 5 a.m., Vikas gestured for a pen and paper. The surgery resident present in the ICU got him one. Vikas wrote for the first time since the accident.

He wrote six words that would break our hearts:

THANK YOU FOR SAVING MY LIFE.

The resident held onto the paper to show it to us later that morning.

Vikas went into cardiac arrest at 6 a.m. that morning.

He was placed back on the ventilators, the cardiac drugs et al. His head, which should have been sunken where the skull wasn't there, was firm. His eyes were still, unresponsive to light and touch.

Vikas was declared brain dead thirteen hours later.

Through his father's anguished face, the endless tears of a bereaved girlfriend and scores of friends, we stood still. We didn't flinch. We were twenty doctors and not one tear. We couldn't afford it. They needed us to support them now, to give them the words of encouragement which would not heal the pain, but would at least keep them going. Even later, when we saw Vikas's last message to us, we didn't lose it. We held firm. It was a piece of paper that hurt worse than a knife. It was a paper no one wanted because of the memories; the number of times we saved him, stayed awake for him, joked with him in a month and took him out of death's door ... only to lose him when the war was over.

We talked a lot that midnight over coffee. About miracles and how elusive they are and about a lesson we had to learn the hard way: how everything you work for can come crashing down in a minute, whether it is our dreams, our pride or simply our God complex.

But then we rise up again, like a phoenix from its ashes, and go all out to do what we are meant to — save lives. Reinstate our dreams, our pride — sans the god complex.

Dr Roshan Radhakrishnan

10

IN GOOD HANDS

In the sick room, ten cents' worth of human understanding equals ten dollars' worth of medical science.

–Martin H. Fischer

A Cup of Milk

It was 9 p.m. and dinner was served in the dining room. Ma was engrossed in watching her favourite television serial along with Kanchan, the teenage girl who was her man-Friday at home. Baba was in his clinic, passionately explaining to his patients the advantages of brushing teeth regularly at night. Meanwhile, I was trying to get the family to the table in time for dinner.

Ours was the home of a dental surgeon, who had begun his career about fifty years ago. My Baba is a self-made man. Born into a family of wealthy zamindars, his concern was never about making money but on acquiring knowledge.

Baba spent his childhood in a remote village in the midst of rice fields, dotted with mango trees, jackfruit orchards and several ponds. My brother and I grew up hearing stories about the struggles of a boy who traversed the thorny path from a village school to a dental college in Kolkata — the long walks to school, the piercing hunger of a growing child on the walk back home, learning English from a dictionary, the beatings he got from the griha shikshak (residential tutor), and studying through the night with a kerosene lamp as companion.

He would relate to us his novel way of staying up at night to study: climbing up a tree and slithering all the way down; it severely grazed his chest and the resultant pain helped keep him awake! Those days there were no anxious parents burning the midnight oil with their kids so they would score the highest in school; the onus was always on the children to pave their own path, the parents were there for love and support. Baba's idol was his Kaka Babu, who was not only his uncle but also his mentor, teacher, guide and inspiration.

After their marriage fifty-three years ago, Baba and Ma travelled to Sambalpur (a small town in Orissa) with a tin trunk and a bedding roll. Baba had taken up a government job in Orissa and his first posting was in Burla Medical College, Sambalpur. Over the years, with a son and a daughter, a flourishing practice and growing fame as a renowned dental surgeon, he got transferred from Sambalpur to Puri, and then finally to the capital city, Bhubaneswar.

We grew up with a loving but forgetful father whose life revolved around his patients. In fact, it was sometimes his patients who would remind him that his children were having examinations at school. Often his assistant would come searching for us: 'Rani, Sonu Babu, Baba is calling the two of you.' Abandoning the mischief at hand we would rush to his clinic. Baba would be in his apron and surgical mask with instruments poised above the mouth of the gaping patient. He would ask, 'Is it true that your final examinations are on? I hope both of you are putting in your best.' The patient would grunt something like a submissive apology for rendering this piece of information and the surgery would continue. However, despite his busy schedule, Baba found the time to play carom or a game of cards with us; he used to run his clinic from home.

My brother is now a cardiologist and settled in Kolkata with his paediatric wife and a cricketer son. I am married with two kids, and have just got transferred to Mumbai. It was my children's summer vacation and I was visiting my parents' place for the breather that every home-maker needs to sustain herself through the rest of the year.

It was almost thirty minutes past nine when all of us sat down for dinner. Grandma's incessant storytelling ensured the diligent tucking in of food by my son and daughter. The dinner was just about finished when Ma said, 'Kanchan, where is my bowl of milk? You know I have one chapatti with warm milk every day, why haven't you kept it ready?' Total silence ensued. We waited for Kanchan's response, but that did not come. Baba shifted in his chair. Ma got up and went to the kitchen and found the milk container washed clean. We heard Kanchan saying softly, 'Ma, Babu has given that milk to his patient.'

Ma returned shaking her head in resignation and acceptance. Baba was not only a doctor; he was like a guardian angel to all his patients. He never discriminated between his rich and poor patients; on all he showered his stern, loving discipline. He called himself a rustic villager who was very particular about people keeping their appointments. He taught us and his patients the value of time and the importance of being punctual. He did not hesitate to turn away an elite person for failing to keep an appointment, and instead attend to the underprivileged patient who had been waiting.

Baba always tried to generate an awareness of dental hygiene among his patients. He would even draw sketches of a tooth with its crown, enamel, gums and nerves to explain the dental condition to his patients, who may have come with a toothache but would go back with a thorough dental check-up.

Baba used to say, 'When a patient comes to me with a dental problem, it is my duty to not only treat the problem but also to check the rest of his teeth.' Money was never his goal. He waived the fees of needy patients who only had blessings and gratitude to give him. Our home always had an abundance of food — cooked/uncooked fish, tiger prawns, sweets, cakes or even jackfruits — Baba wouldn't hesitate to feed these to his needy and hungry patients.

It was not just that cup of milk which made an impression on my mind that day but the dedication of a doctor to treat his patient in every way that he could. Baba had offered the cup of milk to a poor patient that evening before extracting his tooth.

Doctors like him are rare in today's world.

Bipasha Roy

A Doctor's Legacy

'Who is that elderly man sitting on the bench outside?' asked the dentist. I bit my lip. I had deliberately asked Papa to wait outside. 'He's my father,' I replied.

'Oh, why didn't you introduce him to me? What does he do?'

I hesitated for a second but I knew it was no use lying now. 'He's a paediatrician, a former professor of paediatrics at Baroda Medical College. He's retired now.'

The dentist immediately made a beeline for my father and led him to a sofa inside his room. 'Sir,' he said to my father, 'I am sorry I didn't approach you earlier. Can we have a cup of tea together?'

The reason why I had been 'hiding' my father was because when most doctors found out that he was a doctor and had taught at the Baroda Medical College, they refused to charge their consultation fee. They obviously held their alma mater and especially their professors in high regard. As I had feared, the dentist didn't charge his fee, despite protests from me and my father.

'This is embarrassing. I wish they wouldn't do that,' I lamented on our way back home.

My father smiled, patted my head and said, 'Don't worry; we will pay him back in some way or the other. But what I worry about are my countless poor patients, who can't afford to go to a private clinic but sometimes end up being there. I hope the doctors are kind and considerate to them. I hope they remember the lessons learnt at their medical school.'

I knew what my father was talking about; the hospital where my father had worked was what the locals would call a sarkari (government) hospital where medical care was provided free of charge.

I remember my father once buying a stainless steel vessel because a patient, whom he had advised to eat porridge every day after being discharged, had confided that he didn't have a proper cooking utensil. I had once seen my father and his colleagues consoling a weeping mother (whose child had been diagnosed with tuberculosis), explaining patiently to her that it was curable and that she could avail the free nutritious meals provided by the hospital for tuberculosis patients until he was cured. That day, I witnessed the Hippocratic Oath being practiced in its true spirit.

The hospital where he worked was overcrowded. Spread over a sprawling campus and devoid of any elaborate interiors, it was essentially a very humble place. It was always in need of funds and there was a lot of scope for improvement. But there I also saw in the doctors the spirit of unfailing devotion towards their patients. Since it was also a part of the medical college, it was always hoped that the interns would take a leaf out of their professors' lives and go on to become considerate and devoted doctors, and also not forget that the majority of India's population lived below the poverty line.

In the evenings, after my father returned home, we would always have someone or the other seeking a medical opinion — a rickshawalla who would call on 'Shah Sahib' to ask him why his three-month-old son wasn't gaining weight, or the neighborhood maid who wanted to know whether her son had chicken pox. My father had instructed my mother and me to never turn away any patient who came to our door.

When my father died a few years later, we had a lot of visitors — former patients, colleagues and students who were now well-established doctors. One evening, a group of paediatricians came home; they held a silver and blue coloured frame with the words, 'A Tribute to a Great Teacher and a Doctor', printed on it.

One of them said, 'I learnt how to treat my patients with respect, have patience, and compassion for the underprivileged. I learnt all of this from your father.'

'I honed my clinical skills in that hospital but more than that, I learnt never to forget what it really meant to be a human being and a doctor. Our professors never forgot their Hippocratic Oath or got lost in the rat race,' said another.

'I learnt how to listen, how not to dismiss a patient's worries but to empathise with them. I keep a list of trust-funded hospitals with me and when a patient can't afford a procedure, I direct them to hospitals where they can avail it for free. I had seen your father doing this and it has stayed with me,' said a third.

As they began to regale us with tales from the hospital and my father's contributions, I realised that there will always be a breed of doctors who will give unbiased medical advice, refrain from overcharging their patients and respond in the best way they can to those who need them but can't afford their fees.

As I placed the frame next to my father's photograph, I whispered, 'Don't worry, Papa, some lessons are never forgotten ... your legacy continues.'

Prerna Shah

An Early Diagnosis

Let me make a confession: I am scared, yes, truly and terribly scared of doctors. It sounds silly and childish from a grey-haired woman. My post-graduate students, who always trod warily around their stern Director, may even refuse to believe me. But it's the truth, and except for when I was pregnant, I have avoided going to the doctor in all my thirty-two years of marriage.

This is quite unlike my husband, an Air Force officer, who even after retirement goes faithfully for his annual medical check-up. This time, he suggested that I too should get one done; I had reached the grand age of fifty and entered the blissful stage of menopause, or so I thought, when suddenly my monthly cycles re-started on its own. When this happened thrice, my husband dragged me, almost kicking and screaming, to the nearest MI (Medical Inspection, in Air Force parlance) room. As expected, the Air Force doctor put me through a gamut of tests — blood, urine, BP, ECG — and much to my relief, pronounced me fit and fine.

'But,' he added sombrely, 'while this could be normal premenopausal symptoms, I suggest you consult a gynaecologist at the Military Hospital (MH).' When I stubbornly stated that I hated the prodding and probing by gynaecologists, and more so because at MH they were usually male, he found an easier solution. 'At least, get an ultrasound done,' he said.

My relief however, did not last long. As the scanner glided over my gelled abdomen, the radiologist found a hazy mass near my ovaries, and insisted that it needed the attention of a gynaecologist. It was late in the afternoon when we reached the gynaecology department, and the receptionist informed us that no more appointments would be given for the day. Relieved, I turned to escape, when a quiet voice interrupted from behind. 'Is there any problem, Ma'am?'

I turned to see a diminutive young doctor in the olive green uniform of the Army Medical Corps. His name tag proclaimed him to be Captain Dey.

'No problem at all. I'd just come for a general check-up because the radiologist asked me to. I'm fine otherwise, and I can always come back another day,' I blabbered, trying to escape.

But the young Captain would not let me go so easily. He insisted on seeing my report, expressed annoyance that I had never had an examination done before, and was adamant that I have one right away. 'I would prefer a lady or at least a more senior doctor,' I protested.

'I'm the only one available right now,' he said indicating the examination table. Yes, there was a largish growth, he confirmed, and wrote out a long list of tests. I was still in a state of denial and loudly demanded a more senior doctor's advice. At that moment, one did come in. He checked me and pronounced me hale and hearty. 'You can go, Ma'am. Come back after six months for another check-up.'

But the diminutive Captain Dey would not give up.

'Sir, I strongly feel that this needs immediate surgery, and she should go for the necessary pathology and radiology tests.' We were all stunned — in the Army, you never contradict a senior officer, and here was a Captain doing exactly that! And though, at that point of time, I was annoyed at his insistence, later I was to be thankful for it.

The next six weeks went by in a flurry of tests — some of them long and excruciatingly painful. But the results were strangely confusing. The endometrial biopsies and dozens of blood tests gave me a clean chit of health, but not the MRI and the internal ultrasound.

'It has all the signs of a malignant lesion,' pronounced one radiologist.

'It is undoubtedly ovarian cancer,' said the second one, after doing an internal ultrasound.

My world came crashing down. Say what you will, the very word 'cancer' strikes terror into the bravest heart, and I was no brave-heart anyway. Would I die, I thought.

The senior-most gynaecologist calmed me as he gave the verdict: 'Whether it is cancer or not, at this age, we cannot risk leaving a cyst on your ovaries. We'll operate at the earliest. The cyst will be sent for a histo-pathological test after it's taken out, to determine the next course of action.'

The very next day I was admitted to the hospital, and a complete hysterectomy was performed. It was a long operation and recovery was painful. But good news — it was not cancer, though a close shave, as all the doctors and nurses pronounced.

There was every chance that a few more months would not have allowed it to remain benign. 'It's come out at the right time,' was the verdict.

'How did you find out?' they all asked. 'Not everyone is so lucky. Ovarian cancer has hardly any symptoms, and by the time they appear, it's usually too late to save the patient.'

'Ask Captain Dey,' I replied, truly grateful now for both his diagnosis and his persistence. Had it not been for his tenacity, I would have gone back home that day.

'But where is he?' I asked, realising that I'd not seen him ever since the day he had stood up to his senior officer, insisting that my case needed immediate action.

'He has gone on posting; that was his last day in office here,' was the reply.

I was stunned. This young doctor had showed up at the right time and at the right place, with the right attitude. I may never meet him again, but wherever he is, I send him my gratitude and best wishes. He is a shining beacon of what it takes to be a good doctor.

And yes, although doctors may seem fearsome and also inflict some pain, it is a part of the treatment and the cure.

Mita Banerjee

Doctor Do-Little Versus Doctor Do-a-Lot

We always want someone who will do something, just anything, to stem whatever is ailing us — mental or physical. But there is a subtle distinction between a doctor who does nothing and someone who does a little, as and when required.

When my younger sister was diagnosed with leukaemia a few years ago, we got to meet a lot of doctors — good and bad. One of the doctors informed us brusquely of her prognosis without mincing words in our very first meeting with him.

'I wouldn't bother to even try, if I were you. The average mortality rate leaves patients dead in a few months.' We left the room with the feeling that the ground had been whisked away from under our feet and the sky was about to fall on our heads.

Luckily for us, our family doctor held our hand and steadied us. He explained the disease, consoled us, and gave us hope. Then he guided us to the leading specialist in the field, and this is what that doctor had to say:

'Let's start and take it as it comes. Each person is unique and reacts differently, so we'll wait and see.'

Of course, in today's world, we are all cynical about the world of medicine. Do we really need the advised procedure or does the hospital just want to make money? But the point here is that one does not shout out to a drowning man that he is drowning. The best doctors are those who temper their knowledge and experience with humanity and compassion.

It is also true that we choose doctors according to our own temperament. My paediatrician reacts slowly and steadily to the frequent illnesses the kids seem to pick up from god-knows-where. He, and hence I, are masters of the 'art of steam inhalation' — something that has made me the butt of many jokes, even by my husband.

But it is these simple, time-tested and robust remedies that work best anyway. And I am fortunate that my doctor is wise enough to understand this and not pump my kids with medicine at every opportunity. This can however be very frustrating for someone who likes action and an aggressive approach. And so we choose our doctors based on what we want them to do, and not strictly on how 'good' they are.

My sister went through a whole year of painful, invasive treatment. There was about thirty per cent chance that she would make it and she gave it her best shot. The doctors — and there were a battery of them — led us through the entire rigmarole with patience, warmth and a sense of humour. They explained the processes in detail, and honestly and humanely dealt with our fears and doubts. They tried their best to allow her some semblance of normal life.

After many months of treatment and a few cancer-free months, my sister had a relapse. There were a few last-ditch experimental treatments that were being bandied around —

some of the team (who had not worked closely with her) were recommending that we try them. After all, what did we have to lose?

But my sister had had enough. The end was near and the same specialist did what he could to ensure that my sister died a death of dignity. Together, we decided to stop any further treatment and turned our attention to getting her the best palliative care we could find, so that when we did lose my sister, it was a loss that we could see mirrored on these doctors' faces. She was not just a patient, she had become their friend.

In the end, we are all human beings first — and doctors or engineers or scientists later.

Zainab Sulaiman

Knowledge Shield

It was a Friday afternoon and I had just returned from a frenzied business tour. Hot and sultry weather does take its toll and despite the best travel and hotel arrangements, it does make one feel lethargic. Also after a hectic week, wanting to rest on Friday, though a working day, seemed justified.

So as I lay listening to soft music in the cool confines of my room reading an extremely interesting book, I felt like a contented and happy soul. At that instant the door bell rang, and I intuitively felt that there was something wrong. I heard a lady's voice talking urgently to my wife, and it seemed like an emergency. Our flat was on the eighth floor, and she said that a neighbour staying in a flat on the sixth floor had collapsed.

I took the stairs and ran towards the flat. As I entered the main door I saw the lady of the house lying motionless on the floor. By then a few more ladies had reached the house and the worried look on their faces scared me. They all looked at me — it was afternoon and there was no other man around, and I realised I was expected to handle the situation.

Outwardly looking calm, I checked her breathing and then the pulse, which though a bit feeble seemed normal to me. I was also wondering what could be the reason behind this sudden fainting spell. I poured a few drops of cold water on her face and was relieved to see her slowly opening her eyes, and then suddenly sitting up with eyes wide open, as if waking up from deep sleep.

Seeing so many people around she seemed surprised and I explained to her that she had lost consciousness for a brief moment, probably because of exhaustion, and that there was nothing to worry about. While I talked to her, I observed her carefully and was convinced that everything was fine. She was soon normal and started chatting and laughing as though nothing had happened.

During this entire hullabaloo, someone had also called a local doctor who examined the patient and declared that everything was fine — her breathing, pulse and blood pressure were normal. We thanked the doctor, and by that time, her husband had also arrived from office.

He had been informed about the incident over the phone and before leaving his office had also called the family physician. Incidentally we had the same physician and while most people, including the lady who had fainted, felt there was no need of a second opinion, we both were of the belief that an all-clear sign from our physician, Dr Raghu, was necessary.

Dr Raghu is a tall, energetic and cheerful person. Half the trouble melts when he addresses the patient in a tone that injects energy into the psyche. While maintaining eye contact with his patient, he listens intently; Dr Bernard Lown, the

Nobel Prize winner for peace in his famous book *The Lost Art of Healing* has laid lot of emphasis on listening skills and compassion in medical practice. Dr Raghu is a living example of this book's essence. He often says that it is not the doctor but the patient who gives the diagnosis to the doctor.

He examined the lady meticulously and kept on cajoling her to talk more. Finally he scribbled a few words on the paper, reading which I was taken aback. He had suggested a CAT scan of the brain, and wanted the investigation to be done at the earliest.

By late evening the result of the scan had arrived and it confirmed what Dr Raghu had suspected — a brain tumour. With references provided by Dr Raghu, the family rushed to Mumbai the next day, leaving their three school-going daughters under our care. On the third day, we received the news of a successful surgical removal of the tumour .

It has been more than ten years now since the operation, and the lady is in good health. I often shudder to think what would have happened if we had ignored the fainting episode and the timely diagnosis had not been done.

Sanjeev Trivedi

My Wonderful Vaidya

When I first visited Bangalore in 2003, I fell in love with the city. Everything about it was attractive — the weather, the energy, the pace of life, the face of the city. I wanted to settle there for the rest of my life. I came back home to Nagpur with these dreams and one nightmare — severe hair loss.

I couldn't figure out just exactly why my hair had decided to stage an exodus after my return from Bangalore ... did the water not suit me? Was it something I ate? Was it a terminal disease? I fretted over it for a few days before deciding to seek medical help. And this time I headed straight to Dr Deopujari, an Ayurvedic vaidya.

I explained my problem and silently prayed the prognosis would be good ... that I wasn't suffering from cancer or something. The doctor heard me out patiently and then sat down to write a prescription. He asked me for my name. And when he heard it, he said, 'You have come to me before, for getting treatment for jaundice, haven't you?'

It was when I was twelve years old that I was struck by severe jaundice. My bilirubin was 8.4 while the normal value was 1.6. I may have landed up in hospital except we chose to go to an Ayurvedic doctor for treatment — Dr Deopujari. He said there was no need to admit me but bed rest would definitely be required. He wrote out medicines and a long list of diet restrictions. The medicines included raw castor juice on an empty stomach in the mornings, and to a twelve-year-old and her sister, who had a milder bout of jaundice, it did not sound like the best taste to wake up to.

But he looked at both of us and said, 'You know what, you can have rasgullas every single day … lots of them.' And that made up for the terrible medicine he was prescribing for the morning. Little did we realise that the curdled milk from which rasgulla is made would do us jaundice patients a world of good.

With his medicines and by strictly following his diet instructions, my bilirubin came down to normal in less than four weeks. But more than the treatment, it was the way he would talk to us and connect with us kids who couldn't eat anything normal for almost two months. He would try and put a positive spin on anything he was recommending, allowing us a toffee or two every now and then, and helped keep our spirits up even while we were suffering.

When I saw that Dr Deopujari remembered me and my medical history even after six years, I knew I was in good hands. From that day on, I put all my faith in him and let him take over the care of my health completely. He would not only prescribe Ayurvedic medicines for my maladies, but also tell me simple home remedies that would keep unnecessary medical intrusion at bay.

For instance, it is from him that I learnt that a decoction of coriander seeds effectively rids the body of deep-seated fever and it is the only remedy I have used for fever in the last seven-eight years, always experiencing relief in about two hours.

Even when I moved to Bangalore after my graduation and took up a job and residence here, I would call Dr Deopujari back in Nagpur when I was really ill. He would listen to all my symptoms and patiently ask more questions before prescribing some medicines that I would take religiously.

Needless to say I would be blessed with better health in a matter of days and my faith would strengthen further. In going beyond the case at hand and showing enough concern to remember my medical history and tendencies, he proved that he would always choose treatment that was best for me. He has been the ideal doctor for me and I thank him for patiently for treating all those problems, big and small, that I went to him with. I owe my health and confidence in holistic medicine to him.

Anupama Kondayya

The Doctor on Green Street

It was 3 a.m. when I sensed my daughter, Vinita, sitting up in bed. Turning on the light, I saw her huddled, breathing hard and in great pain.

'Is it your stomach?' I asked. She shook her head and pointed to her ears. We were relatively new to that part of Mumbai, having settled there a just a year before, in 1977. I called up my cousin who gave me a phone number and also offered to accompany us to Dr Vaishnav's on Green Street. 'He's a general practitioner,' he said, 'and a good one.'

My son, Vikky, fetched a cab and within ten minutes we were on Green Street. The lights were on at Dr Vaishav's ground-floor flat. He first listened to us before he examined Vinita's ear, and then said 'wax'. He went inside and within minutes, emerged with a syringe. There was a suppressed yell from Vinita, after which she began to smile.

'How much do we owe you, Doctor?'

'That will be twenty rupees,' he said. That was all. That was the first time we met Dr Vaishnav. He was simple and a man of few words. His only interest seemed to be in restoring his patients to normal health. We often saw him cycling energetically, visiting patients in the neighbourhood. Thereafter, we sought him out every time we needed medical help. He normally gave us tablets and a mixture from the three bottles that stood on his shelf.

'Take that for three days,' he would say cryptically.

'How much do we owe you, Doctor?'

'It is rupees ten for consultation and rupees ten for the medicine.'

'Should we come back in three days?'

'Why? You'll be fine by then.'

A few years later, we saw crayon scribbles on the walls of his clinic. We looked at him curiously. 'My twin grand-daughters enjoy drawing and I hate to stop them. Walls can be easily painted again,' he remarked with a smile.

My husband who had accompanied me to the clinic for the first time, pointed to a large propeller standing in a corner of the room. A discreet question revealed that flying had been the doctor's hobby in his younger days. Subsequently, we discovered that his interests had no limitations. He had learnt Reiki, a Japanese touch-healing technique, and now was a Reiki Master. Many of his patients were cured with Reiki. He even practiced pranic healing and studied astrology.

A close relative of ours had not conceived even after five years of marriage despite a prolonged course of treatment. We suggested that she meet Dr Vaishnav. He asked for her horoscope and assured her that she would have a child the following year — and she did. A friend of ours with a severe stomach problem had consulted two specialists, and both had advised surgery. Having heard about Dr Vaishav she begged us to accompany her to his clinic. After examining her, he walked over to his shelf and gave her some tablets and a mixture. His charges were just twenty rupees. He assured her that she would be fine in three days. She has been perfectly fit for the last twelve years without surgery.

One day the doctor called up with a mysterious message. 'Tell Kalpana the date will be 2nd or 3rd January, without any complications.' He hung up before I could ask him what he meant. When my daughter-in-law, Kalpana, returned home, I gave her the message and she laughed with relief. Her baby was due on 12th January and she had feared she might have to undergo a caesarian. She had voiced her fears to the doctor. He had looked at the clock and said he'd consult the 'prashna kundali' — a branch of astrology which helps answer a question posed at a particular time of the day. As it turned out, our grandson arrived at 8.30 p.m. on 2nd January, without surgical intervention.

Dr Vaishnav, our miracle man, has retired now, but when no other medication helps, we do consult him on the phone. As always, he comes up with a simple remedy that works like magic. When we call him up again to give him the feedback, we hesitantly ask him about the consultation fees. He says he has retired and therefore charges nothing. When we insist, he says, 'Oh … are you okay, now? Fine, send the amount by telephone!' and the line goes dead.

Savitri Babulkar

The Flip Side

The medical profession is amongst the most respected professions in this world and ironically it is also one of the most maligned. Depending on our experiences, we either idolise doctors or make villains out of them. An incident in my life made me come across two doctors — one, I remember for his compassion and timely help, and the other for just the opposite reasons.

I distinctly remember that day. It was late afternoon, and I was relaxing in my room with a magazine. My son was lying next to me reading a book. Suddenly, he started tickling me and we got into a pillow fight. He then ran out of the room and I pursued him playfully. He entered another room and shut the door. I waited with bated breath for him to open it. As soon as he opened the door, I tried to catch hold of him, and in order to avoid me, he banged the door shut again. What followed will be etched in my memory forever. I shrieked with pain. When I looked at my hand, I was horrified to see that the tip of my little finger had been sliced off.

I became hysterical and started hunting for the part that had been severed. Later, on finding it, I rushed along with my sister to the closest hospital. I was in agonising pain and devastated at having lost a precious part of me, which my poor sister now held in a small plastic pouch. On reaching the hospital, I requested the authorities to take me to the doctor in charge of emergencies. The callous attitude of the hospital authorities was unbelievable. Being exposed to so many accidents every day had obviously de-sensitised them to my traumatic condition.

The doctor-in-charge again turned out to be the proverbial devil. He was surprisingly rude, and instead of seeing me immediately, he condescendingly agreed to see me only after he had attended to all his other follow-up cases. My distress knew no bounds; my sister called up a friend in the medical profession, who instantly asked us to rush to another big hospital in our vicinity.

On reaching there, I was immediately taken to the OPD and given the required first aid. Meanwhile, my husband and other relatives had reached there and in a short while, an emergency surgery was performed on my finger. This was done sometime around midnight, far beyond the working hours of the doctor, who could have chosen to comfortably relax in bed rather than try to mend my little finger. However, he chose the call of duty over his comfort and very carefully and patiently stitched up my finger. He was sensitive and reassuring.

Today, no one can really make out the difference between my mended finger, and the other ones. The stitches have dried up, the wounds have healed, but the contribution of both the doctors in my life that day will remain with me forever.

Ektaa Rupani

The Philosopher Who Cares

There is a doctor in Pune whose true calling lies in caring for the elderly. Dr D offers ease to the dying simply by being there and holding their hand as they pass into the next world. But often enough he pulls them back from the brink of death, and returns them to as active a life as their fragile bodies will permit. While they heal he takes time out to discuss philosophy with his patients. He trains people in geriatrics, counsels them when stressed, offers solutions for their problems, and discusses the latest advances in geriatric medicine. Dr D is always available in an emergency; he never ever made us feel he was in a hurry to go somewhere else.

My mother-in-law had suffered memory loss for several years, and now the stress of Papa's illness had tipped her into dementia. It was obvious she could not cope with looking after even herself. The hospital doctor suggested cryptically that I had a long-term problem to deal with. So it was decided that once Papa was fit to travel they would move to our house.

Dr D reviewed Papa's medication, and discarded a stockpile of tablets which once prescribed had never been discontinued.

Just after that Papa suffered from an acute urinary infection. At the same time, Ma started going out for walks and would vanish for hours together. We worried that she might get lost.

Dr D arranged for day and night nurses for Papa, and suggested a day ayah for Ma. At first we resisted this idea, but as Papa's health became worse, we engaged an elderly Maharashtrian lady whom everyone called Aaji. While Papa hovered between life and death, too sick to be even moved to hospital (which he did not want anyway), Aaji took over Ma, taking her for walks, supervising her bathing and dressing, and keeping her occupied.

I had not expected to have two patients to take care of, and without Dr D's help I could never have managed it. Our home had suddenly become a hospital, but he was so supportive, so willing to just sit and talk, I hardly felt the burden. Even when he came three times a day he charged us for only a single visit. He taught me to give injections, to recognise an emergency before it happened, found us a physiotherapist who would come home, and even an ophthalmologist to come and check Papa's eyesight once he was better. For he got better!

One morning, after several days of delirium, during which his long-dead cousin Bansi visited him at night and sat on his bed (I wondered if he had come to escort my father-in-law to the next world), Papa called weakly to me. His eyes were clear, and his breathing was better. I felt his pulse; his skin was cool.

'Did I die?' he asked me.

'No,' I said, 'you are very much alive.'

'I thought Bansi came to see me,' he said.

'He went back,' I said.

'Yes,' said Papa thoughtfully. 'He said he was going. But he said he would come again.'

The night Bansi had 'visited' us I had, at Papa's urging, prepared a cup of tea for our invisible guest. As it was at three in the morning, it was an eerie experience that still gives me the goose-bumps. Dr D said that (in his view) it was not unusual for the dead to visit the dying, so that they would not depart this world alone. A fascinating idea! We had many discussions about life and death that crossed the borders of our three religions, for I was a Christian, married to a Hindu, while our good doctor was a Muslim.

Thereafter Papa had urinary problems from time to time, though never as serious as the first time. Dr D thought a tight foreskin might be the source of infection, and decided that a slit to loosen it would solve the problem. But Papa refused to go to the hospital.

'I will die in hospital,' he said. 'Do it here.'

Dr D persuaded a surgeon to perform the operation at home. The bedroom became an operating theatre. Papa insisted that I sit next to him and hold his hand. Kusum, our nurse, checked his pulse. Dr D stood at the foot of the bed. My husband sat out of the way in a corner. Our white cat stalked in and out like a hospital matron. It could not have been more public, but Papa, happily sedated, did not care. In the middle of it all the power went off; the operation was completed by the light of two emergency lamps, three oil lamps and a pocket torch. For a couple of weeks the wounded foreskin was covered with a small piece of sterile gauze, which Papa called his diaper. He teased the doctor that his attempt to circumcise him had not succeeded! It became a joke between them. It certainly seemed to solve the problem; Papa recovered well, and lived happily without further infection for another two years.

Then one day, after a pleasant lunch with two of our friends, Papa had a choking fit which quickly turned into a full-blown heart attack. While Kusum got him into bed, I called Dr D and then frantically tried to call my husband, who was out of town on business.

Papa caught my hand, whispering Bansi's name, while looking at the corner of the room. Even as the doctor checked his pulse, his breathing slowed and rattled, his face became waxen, and he was gone. Bansi had collected his boyhood companion.

Dr D wrote the death certificate. We called all our relatives and the funeral was arranged. My husband came back just in time to perform the last rites. Dr D stayed with us till the body was consigned to the flames. Next day he came to check on Ma. There was no bill for his last services to Papa.

Six months later my husband had a heart attack, which he survived — just. Four days after the bypass surgery, he died of an unsuspected gastric ulcer, which had perforated. Dr D was there, supporting, counseling, till the last rites were performed by our son and the last mourner had departed. After a few weeks Ma went to live with my brother-in-law. Now I was alone.

For most of my life I had cared for people, and had never lived alone. Until I had sorted out my life, until I moved to live near my children, Dr D phoned me frequently, every day at first, and never charged me for the calls.

We meet from time to time. After almost fifteen years he is still the philosopher who always has time to discuss religion, life and death, this world and the next. He has a roaring practice with the elderly. He suits them: who else would find time to talk of such things in this busy life? But Dr D understands that they have time on their hands, a wealth of accumulated wisdom, and deep philosophical questions to debate upon. He gives them a chance to enjoy these things — he gives them a reason to live.

Jane Bhandari

The Stitch

My daughter had met with a serious accident and her hand was completely damaged. There was a deep gash between her fingers which had cut her hand almost in two.

I got to know of this only after a couple of weeks when I returned home from an official tour. As my wife narrated the incident, I could only see the sobbing face of my daughter. I was aghast; how had she gone through that pain, she who would shriek for even a small injection!

I went into my daughter's room. She was fast asleep; I stared at her for a few moments, saw her bandaged hand and then left the room without disturbing her. I wished to talk to her and impatiently waited for morning to arrive. I was full of guilt for not being there when she had needed me, but was proud of my strong wife who had dealt with the situation on her own. I was also grateful to the doctor who had treated her. I spent a sleepless night, and woke up next morning to find her seated at the dining table drinking her coffee.

With a charming smile, she said, 'How was your trip, Pops?'

'Bad, we didn't get the contract,' I replied.

Gradually we started discussing how she had met with the accident and she told me how badly her middle finger was bruised. I got to know that she had twenty-one stitches on a single finger. To my surprise, most of our conversation was about the doctor, not about the pain and suffering she must have undergone. I too was eager to meet the doctor after listening to my wife and daughter.

When I did meet the doctor, I didn't find him at all different from the other doctors. He was calmly listening to his patients, directing his assistants to get one or the other report, and in no hurry to see the next patient. We exchanged greetings and then I said, 'Thank you so much for being so patient with my soft-hearted daughter, who is fearful of injections even at the age of twenty-two.'

The doctor turned and said quietly to my daughter, 'Didn't you tell your father you were watching me while your hand was getting stitched?' And my daughter said, 'No, I forgot.'

Then he said to me, 'Mr Batra, your daughter is strong although she did shriek when I gave her the anaesthesia before the stitches.'

I was amazed at the rapport between my daughter and Dr Awadhi; I would take her to the doctor every fourth or fifth day for the dressings and each time he removed a few stitches from her hand.

And then came the final day we were waiting for, when the remaining six stitches would be removed. My daughter was very happy that day, hoping that after almost a month, she would be able to use her hands at last.

She was waiting eagerly for 7 p.m., when we had our appointment with Dr Awadhi. He took off her bandage and examined her hand, then silently cut only two stitches and again started wrapping it up. My daughter was disappointed and shouted, 'Why are you not taking out the rest of the stitches?' Tears slipped down her cheeks.

Dr Awadhi said, 'It needs more time to heal.'

She started whimpering, 'You can never understand how it feels to wait for others to perform your basic tasks; I feel so troubled to ask others all the time.'

After that emotional visit, we didn't exchange a word all the way home. She was weeping; and we knew it was not because of the pain or the stitches, but because of the helplessness she was experiencing. After some time, she reached for her phone and told us that she should say sorry to the doctor as she had yelled at him.

But when she looked at her phone, she was surprised to read the message on the screen. It was from the doctor, and said, 'I am sorry but I just can't do that. You have to wait for a few days. Sorry, dear.'

I was amazed that despite being so busy, he had taken time to soothe someone's pain and disappointment.

Pranit Paras

11

THE HEALING PROCESS

Drugs are not always necessary. Belief in recovery always is.

–Norman Cousins

A Homeopathic Experience

I went to see this doctor for two reasons; firstly, he was very good looking and secondly, he had asked me to keep at least two hours free! That I had a chronic health problem was an insignificant matter in comparison!

A doctor — young, with two hours to spare and a Homeopath; any sensible person would say, 'No way, don't waste your time!' But if anyone has taken the poet Frost seriously, it is me, and so I decided to take the road less travelled.

For the first ten minutes, I briefed him about my condition. Then I confessed as to how I myself play doctor by mixing Ayurveda medicines with Naturopathy and Allopathy but had yet to strike the right combination.

He did not react. Instead, he asked me, 'What is the exact nature of your problem? Can you describe it?'

I explained in detail.

'Please do not mind, but can you describe your pain a little more?' he said.

I took a deep breath; I became aware of the pain and described it in detail to him.

'When you feel good, how do you feel?' he changed the topic.

'I feel connected, to the world, to my body, to my breath,' I said.

'Can you describe this happy, connected feeling?'

'I can breathe properly, I feel a flow of energy and my thoughts slow down. I feel happy.'

'Yes, how do you feel when you're happy?'

'I feel like singing, I dance without music; I look at fresh vegetables in the market and say thank you, Earth.'

'How do you feel in your body when you are happy?' he asked yet again.

I was at a loss for words, and I told him so.

'That is very good. Now describe this feeling of being wordless and tell me more about this connected feeling.'

'Well, I can feel connected even when I am without words.'

'Yes, tell me about this.'

'Well, plants don't talk, but they enjoy as well as suffer silently.'

'Oh, okay ... please explain that.'

'Well, they suffer if you don't water them or if you pluck them,' I explain.

'And how do they enjoy themselves?' He seemed really interested in my rambling.

'They look at the moon all night but they don't tell you about it.'

'So how do you feel when you sense this connection to plants?'

I was beginning to wonder which one of us was a moron. 'I feel good,' I said.

'No, this is your mental reaction. Tell me how you feel in your body.'

'There is no tension; no effort to find the right words ... there is a deep satisfaction. I feel rested and relaxed.'

'That is very good. Now we will discuss the opposite. Tell me about when you feel tense.'

'Well, I feel tense when I am criticised, when there is work pressure, or when I am in a hurry.'

'Give me an example.'

'Well, I can't handle criticism, even constructive criticism.'

'How do you feel when you are criticised?'

'I feel diminished.'

'Diminished? What do you mean by diminished?' (You don't understand English, Doc, right? I said to myself.)

I made a gesture, in which I am squashing a balloon. 'Like this, diminished. Like all my energy, my enthusiasm just dissipates ....'

'Good. Now make that gesture again, and tell me how you feel, when you feel diminished.'

I smiled. But I made that gesture again.

'Yes, tell me how you feel,' he said. I was beginning to respect this young doctor.

'I feel like I am pushed into a dark corner and I can't breathe. I don't have access to my mind, my logical faculties, and so I lash out in anger because anger is the only way I can survive the dark corner.'

'Anger is again a reaction. Tell me what happens in that dark corner, when you can't breathe,' he prodded me further, to go into hell.

'In the dark corner, when I can't breathe, no actually I can breathe but I suppose I am not aware of my breathing.'

'This is your mental understanding. Tell me what happens in that dark corner.' he said.

'I don't feel connected to life. I feel like a stone, separated from everything and everybody.'

'Yes …' he waited.

'Time stands still. I could be a ghost hanging on a tree for ages, who can see everything, but who can't communicate with anyone. Can I share something, doctor?'

'Yes.'

'When I was talking of the happy moments, my pain had gone. And now it is back.'

'That is very good. We are getting there.'

He pulled out a fat book, read for a couple of minutes and found the remedy. 'Take three pills, three times a day. Come back after three days. If this is the right medicine, it will cure the pain.'

As I walked down the steps from his clinic, I made the gesture of squashing a balloon and laughed.

I didn't know if this doctor would actually cure me. But it was such a delight to meet an artist in the disguise of a doctor.

Manjushree Abhinav

A Hug

To be able to look back upon one's life in satisfaction is to live twice.

–Kahlil Gibran

Dr Kapoor was the fourth psychologist I was visiting in a span of three months. He had a home that looked beautiful from the outside, a nice garden and a voice that made me feel at ease. I sat in one of the cane chairs in the waiting area. Those days I didn't feel alive; it was as if I was merely existing. I was hoping that Dr Kapoor would help me change the way I felt.

Yes, I had just been through an emotional roller-coaster ride. I thought life had ended or maybe hoped it would. But, ironically, I was alive. After months of sleepless nights, hours of sobbing and screaming, one night I realised that whatever happens I will still live. There had been nights when I had gone to sleep wishing that I would never see another day again. One night, I firmly told myself that I was going to live and cease merely existing.

I had been pondering over the word 'psychologist' for a while. I searched online and the very next day, I got an appointment with a doctor. He helped me understand that I was going through depression and referred me to a certain Dr A, as his consultation charges were high and I required frequent visits. I thanked him and my faith in myself. I then went to Dr B.

Every week I would find an excuse to get away from my roommates and go to meet him. Not that they did not know about my situation, but they thought I could deal with it with their help. They had always stood by me and believed we could together change my life. I trusted them and knew they would do their best, but I also knew that I needed to be healed. Only my sister Bonnie, who lived with me, knew after a couple of weeks that I regularly sneaked out to see the psychologist.

Meanwhile, my parents thought I should get married to heal my broken heart. The more I refused the more adamant they were about it. Then finally, Bonnie had to tell them that I was seeing a psychologist for my depression. They were shocked; they lived abroad and appointed an aunt of mine (who was a head-nurse then, the only one with some medical knowledge in the family) to take me to a doctor she thought appropriate. I was directed to a doctor, an ex-professor and a retired Head of Department of one of Bangalore's most prestigious mental health institutions.

'Rashmi?' the man in front of me called out. Dr Kapoor was an aged man with silver hair and a pleasant smile.

'Yes, I am Rashmi,' I replied and he welcomed me into his consultation room.

I spoke to him nervously, with tears running down my cheeks. Soon, I was howling in front of him. He heard it all, smiled and then hugged me. He said that my life had not ended and I had to tell myself that I wanted to live.

He prescribed medicines and told me to meet him every fortnight. As I walked out from his clinic, I felt as if a burden was taken off my chest; I felt light and hopeful. I guess what I needed the most was his hug ... it made me feel alive and reminded me I needed it and that I wanted to live ... and love.

I met him every fortnight for the next five months. As weeks passed by the dose of my medications came down. I began to feel good again. After five months of consultations, he announced that he was going abroad to attend a seminar and would be back after a few weeks. By then, my dosages had come down, and once he left, I decided to try and live without the medication. In spite of knowing that a fluctuation in the dosage of psychiatric medication could cause major mood swings and other reactions, I stopped the medication voluntarily.

I seemed to be fine and in a period of three weeks, I was off the medicines! I felt truly happy. I seemed to be strong, confident and open to life and love. I realised that I was not depressed anymore ... I wasn't crying all the time! I was just waiting for Dr Kapoor to come back and hug me!

One night, Bonnie and Maya, my close friends, woke me up around 2 a.m. (by now, a couple of my roommates also knew about my visits to the psychologist) and then they told me that Dr Kapoor had passed away ... he'd had a cardiac arrest.'

The next moment, I felt like I was drowning! I had come such a long way in the past five months ... it had been a huge struggle to overcome the depression and now it felt like I was becoming weak again. Suddenly I realised that my life seemed to have spun around him in the last five months; he had become my anchor, my reason for living! I thought about myself before I met Dr Kapoor and how he had helped me see the positive side of life again. Bonnie and Maya consoled me, but in vain! I sobbed like a baby.

The next day, I was weepy the entire morning and when I looked towards the sun, a light seemed to enter me. Then a voice inside me said, 'You cannot let go, Rashmi. I trusted you so much in the last days of my life. I spent time and energy on you. You cannot let me down. Rise and live. Smile, I like that smile of yours. Make me proud.' And I felt that warm feeling again, as if he was hugging me ... at least I would like to believe that he did.

I have lived every moment of my life ever since. I felt ready to continue with life and got married after four months. Now with my husband and a wonderful daughter, I live like I do not have a tomorrow. Today I can look back at my life and smile.

This life is what it is because of you, Dr Kapoor. A hug from you is all that I needed. I will always be so grateful to you!

Rashmi Balakrishnan

Musical Touch

On a hot summer morning, when I was getting ready to go to work, I slipped in my bedroom. Before I could even get up, I saw my twisted wrist and started howling. I was in great pain and immediately knew that it was a fracture. Fractures were not new to me; I had earlier fractured my leg when I was a student in the university and was confined to my humble bed for almost three months. I always dreaded the pain and agony that come with a fracture. But then there are certain things you don't choose in life but they just happen to you.

Then with great difficulty, I went to the nearest hospital for an X-ray. I was hoping that it would be a minor fracture which would heal quickly. But that summer day, luck was not on my side. The report showed that it was a very complicated fracture, and the hospital made urgent calls to the orthopaedic surgeon. When he looked at my X-ray report, he told me that I had no option but to go for surgery.

The surgery was fixed for five in the evening and the waiting added to my already sagging morale. I kept on cursing my fate and even found faults with the flooring of my home. Between all this, I also thanked God that the fracture involved only my left hand and at least I could move around.

But then hospital visits are not what I look forward to in life and, I guess many people would agree with me. I think the wisest man is the one who said 'heath is wealth'. Even though I was trying to act cool lying on the hospital bed, I was getting butterflies in my stomach in anticipation of my surgery. Far away from my parents and sisters, my confidence level was not too high. How I longed for those days when my father and mother would stand by me even for minor illnesses!

Before the surgery, I had to go through hundreds of tests and once the reports were all fine, I was wheeled into the operation theatre. My surgeon was there with his team. There was a flurry of activity inside the operation theatre. Then my doctor's mobile rang and the ring tone was one of my favourite songs by Kishore Kumar. Even in that moment of pain, it brought a smile on my face.

Music is one of my passions in life and I couldn't help but tell my doctor how much I enjoyed listening to that song. And that broke the ice and he asked me which other songs I liked. He switched off his mobile but the conversation about music continued and it soothed me. And my mind was busy associating memories with our common favourite songs and it transported me to a different world. It eased the mounting tension in my mind.

After my surgery, for many weeks I had to visit him in the clinic for follow-up checks. And every time, our conversation revolved around music and that always eased my pain. Slowly, I was on the path to recovery. Finally the day came when the plaster, which had become my accessory for months, was removed from my hand. There was no need to visit my doctor regularly and I wanted to say a heart-felt thank you to him for making my pain less with his expertise and conversation about music. I picked up a music CD of my favourite singer, Cat Stevens, as a gift for him. He wished me a speedy recovery and we hoped to stay in touch with each other. A few days after that I got an SMS from him which read, 'I am enjoying the songs, and some of my doctor friends want to borrow the CD. Thank you.'

Didn't somebody say music has great healing powers? Only if the healer — the doctor — knows how to use it!

Deepika

The Healing Process

When I fractured my right hand in a scooter accident, the world came to a standstill for me. For an independent woman to have her functional hand rendered temporarily useless was bad enough, but to depend on family members for basic and trivial things like brushing and combing was my worst nightmare come true. Values ingrained in me rebelled at the prospect of sitting there doing nothing while my husband and daughter slogged to keep home and hearth running. Each visit to the doctor's turned into my personal ranting session.

'Why did this happen to me?' became my opening line and I would launch into a monologue elaborating all that had gone wrong with my life. The doctor would listen patiently while changing the dressing on the fracture, murmuring sympathetically at appropriate intervals.

A typical conversation between us went something like this:

Me: 'How could God do this to me?'

Doc: 'Hmmm.'

Me: 'I mean, for a homemaker not to be able to look after her family is a catastrophy.'

Doc: 'Hmmm.'

Me: 'I am unable to cook my daughter's favourite dishes; the house is in shambles; everything is in a mess and I am helpless!'

Doc: 'Hmmm.'

Me: 'Thank you for listening to me, Doc.'

Doc: 'Hmmm.'

I would come away feeling light-hearted but by the next visit all the emotions would accumulate again and I would vent it out at the clinic.

On my fourth appointment with him I was surprised to see three other people sitting in the room.

'Ah, Kala come in,' the doctor greeted me. 'Let me introduce you to Raman,' he said indicating the gentleman standing nearest to me. 'Next to him is Vivek, and that is Sunitha.'

I nodded, confused as to what was going on. The doctor continued, 'Raman runs a hotel, Vivek works in a construction firm and Sunitha is a teacher. We meet every weekend at an NGO where we do voluntary work for special children.'

Then he turned and addressed them, 'Thank you for your valuable time. I shall see you on Sunday at the NGO.'

'What was all that about?' I could not help asking once they had left.

'Did you notice anything unusual about them?' he countered my query.

'No. They looked normal to me,' I replied.

'And did they seem depressed?'

'No not at all,' I said. In fact, in the few minutes that I had spent with them, I could only feel positive vibes emanating from them.

'Good. Now listen to this. Raman lost vision in one eye when he was a child, Sunitha is a breast cancer survivor and Vivek lost his right leg in an accident and is walking on a prosthetic limb.'

I sat there stunned by what I had just heard. Here I was wallowing in a pool of self pity while those three extraordinary people carried on with their lives with infectious optimism.

Doc continued after a pause, 'Kala, I understand your predicament. It is tough for any loving wife and mother to sit idle and watch her family work. But complaining is not the solution, you have to try and focus on the positive. For so many years you have worked tirelessly for your family. Consider this a vacation. Not an ideal way to get rest, I agree, but you have to make the best of the situation. Develop the faculties of your left hand. Read inspirational literature. Watch your favourite comedies. There are so many ways to beat negativity if you focus on it.'

Something shifted inside me after that momentous meeting. Doc had not only expedited the process of mending broken bones, he had also taught me to count my blessings.

Indeed, my fracture healed soon after and my life went back to normal. I owed my newfound optimism to Doc; each time I recalled how he had gone out of the way to help me appreciate life I felt an overwhelming sense of gratitude. To express the same I sent him a simple message: 'Thank you for healing me in more ways than one.'

His reply was prompt. 'You are welcome. I shall send you a separate bill for the motivational discourse I gave the other day!'

Kalaivani Asokan

The Power of Belief

*The thing always happens that you really believe in; and the belief
in a thing makes it happen.*

–Frank Lloyd Wright

As a knee replacement doctor, I have helped many patients walk again. The feeling is amazing when they revisit to thank me or request to be operated on their other knee just by me. I feel humbled and blessed to be chosen by the Lord to restore hope in faded lives again.

I still remember the hardships of my residency period — the sleepless nights, the unending duty hours and the ruthless tone of senior resident doctors to toil harder. Sometimes the pressure was so immense that I would think about quitting. While those were the toughest days of my life, they taught me the importance of determination, patience and love. The love and respect that I got from patients in the ward of Nair Hospital kept my dreams alive and I wanted to be capable enough to cure them.

This happened during my first year as a resident, when I was just a houseman in the general ward of Nair Hospital.

After finishing off my day's work, I was cleaning and preparing the charts of patients when a stretcher rolled into the operation theatre. It was an emergency and I, being the only one around, was asked to assist the senior doctor in the surgery.

The man was in terrible pain as he had dislocated his knee after a fall. The two-hour operation went smoothly and I finally finished the dressing and prepared him to be rolled back to the general ward. I was unnerved to see the anxiety on the faces of his relatives who were waiting outside the OT.

For the next four days my shift happened to be in the same ward. That man was on bed number 303. He seemed to respond to his treatments and medicines, but he had lost all hope that he would walk again.

One afternoon when I was dressing his knee, he held my hand and cried. I sat there and we spoke at length. He made his living by tailoring outfits and was worried about his family as he could not walk, or work again on his leg-operated sewing machine. I tried to explain to him that we can heal a wound with medicines but only belief can cure one completely. My last words to him were, 'Sab theek ho jayega (everything would be all right)', because after that I was shifted to the first floor ward. Now I could no longer meet that man on bed number 303, but would often remember him and pray for his well-being.

Six months later during my rounds in the ward, a man walked up to me. It was the same man from bed number 303 standing tall on his feet, clutching the hands of his little daughter. He could walk again and had resumed work. He had come to thank me for my care and affection.

I was touched by his gesture. Before leaving he stopped to say, 'Doctor Saab, you always said "Sab theek ho jayega", and today I am walking only because I believed you.'

Dr Kalpesh Shah
(As told to Abhilasha Agarwal)

The Subtle Art of Healing

My friend, who is an obstetrician, is the most cheerful human being that I have come across. Her ability to bond with her patients is amazing. It is often typical for patients to be a little scared of their doctors but she is one doctor whom patients feel free to crack jokes with.

She had a patient who underwent an abdominal surgery two months back. In one of the follow-up visits, the patient asked her to see if something was left inside her, while the surgery was being performed.

'What makes you think that?' the surprised doctor asked.

The patient teasingly replied, 'You were so chirpy and talkative during the surgery that I feel you might have forgotten something inside, before stitching me up!'

Of all the various kinds of medical treatment, the most touching and emotional moment is the experience of bringing a new life into this world. The obstetrician is fully aware of the importance the arrival of the baby has in the lives of the parents and relatives, and this is what makes them look after the expectant mother with utmost care. For the same reason, there is considerable anxiety during the delivery. Only when the newborn is found to be safe and healthy does the atmosphere in the labour room become cheerful.

A famous musician was to deliver her first baby and there was a lot of tension in the air. The lady was on an epidural which took care of the pain but kept the patient fully aware of what was happening around her. After a few tense moments, when the baby was born, there was rejoicing in the labour room and my obstetrician friend heaved a sigh of relief. Seeing that both the baby and the mother were safe and secure, she made a peculiar demand to the mother: 'Please sing a song while I complete the rest of the procedure.'

The new mother without hesitation obliged and amidst cheers sang a beautiful song. Both the doctor and the young mother thanked each other for their performance.

It was only during her follow-up visit that the musician laughed and told the doctor, 'I was stunned when you asked me to sing while you completed the procedure. I thought if I didn't follow your instructions, you would goof up, and so I started singing. But as I sang I felt so relieved and happy that I forgot all about the stress of childbirth.'

Healing is an art which my obstetrician friend has mastered.

Sanjeev Trivedi

The Wrong Right

I screened the slide back and forth
As I peeked through the microscope
A furious looking cell stared at me
Eureka! I exclaimed with pride and glee
'Carcinoma' was my undoubted decree.

My adamant colleague refused to agree
He made a mockery of my grey cell ability
And dismissed my verdict with a tinge of hostility
It's just an inflammatory cell, buddy,
As benign as a dead flea!

My expertise doubted, my self-esteem trampled,
A severe blow to my medical arrogance
I took it up as a challenge
My insult I needed to avenge
How can I be proven erroneous?

Both of us sought the counsel of Big Boss
Whose eyes can swoop on a cell like a hawk!

I prayed my belligerent colleague be proven wrong
And my joy knew no bounds when
'It is malignant,' he assertively pronounced.

My battered ego appeased
Out of the hospital stormed an egotist
Ecstatic at being proven a whiz
I deserved to treat myself to a drink
Three cheers for me — an adept pathologist!

On my way I glanced at the lady, frail and old
Awaiting her young son's report with hope
I did not have to notice her, of course
Coz I wasn't going to be the one to give her the news
That her young son had only a few tomorrows.

I sat in my car and pondered where to party that evening
But something gnawed at my heart; an intense ache
Hot tears poured down my cheeks sans warning
And undid the façade I was sporting
The wee bit of a human hidden in me startled my being.

Late into the sleepless night I had a dream
Big Boss admonished me, yet on my face I saw a gleam
A single streak of the whitener fluid he drew
To erase my faulty reporting and write one anew
Do early morning dreams really come true?

Reeta Mani

Trading in Hope

'You will need hospitalisation, I think,' she said with a straight face when I told her about my eye infection. She is a close friend and I looked at her, shocked.

'How do you know?'

'Because I am a doctor,' she answered and we both laughed.

Ruksheeda is an accomplished doctor, a psychiatrist. We are friends, and we often forget our professional lives when we are together. She was right; I had to be hospitalised and during that time she was my pillar of strength. While everyone seemed to be frightened and in the process made me nervous, she was the only one who was practical yet positive.

As we spend a lot of time together, we are pretty good at gauging each other's moods. Of course we discuss the highs and lows in our professional lives but we largely unwind by talking about non-work related things. It helps at times that we are from totally different fields. The other day, we met for dinner and she looked particularly happy, so I was curious and waited for her to tell me the reason. She needed a lot of prodding but then she confided how she felt truly glad that she had chosen medicine as her profession. Now I was truly intrigued.

She told me about R, whom she had met eight years ago. He was a depressed nineteen-year-old with suicidal thoughts. He had come with his parents who were bewildered by his strange behaviour. What had happened to their brilliant boy? He had a bright future and dreams of doing an MBA after completing his engineering degree, but now.....

He was a good-looking boy who thought all of us were wasting his time. He took time to open up. He had led a privileged life and his parents were honest, hard-working professionals. He was good at academics, popular with his friends, yet he was suffering from depression bordering on the paranoia. He believed his grades were falling because of the construction in the neighbour's home which disturbed him and his mother's inability to stop it. Ruksheeda tried to get through to him by building his trust in her. But it was far from easy....

In the interim he became worse and stopped talking to anyone. The panic-stricken parents thought Ruksheeda's restrained approach was worsening things and rushed to another doctor. The boy was put under heavy sedation and soon became a shadow of his old self. A couple of months later they were back at her clinic looking sheepish; R had said he wanted to come and see her. Yet he wouldn't talk.

Finally after much persuasion, he said he wished to speak to her alone. He then told her that he had to finish this course and do his MBA, so she needed to do something or be responsible for his suicide. She guaranteed him her help but he had to follow her instructions and be very strong to get over his illness. He liked that but felt there was little hope that he would get well. Ruksheeda assured him that she had enough hope for both of them.

They were finally making some progress and he was responding positively to the medication, until his uncle from the US came into the picture and decided he needed to see a more expensive, and thus 'better' doctor. His mother pleaded her helplessness and R vanished again. Ruksheeda felt frustrated but there was no way she could argue with his parents beyond a point. So she prayed for him to get better.

For two years she had no clue about him, and then one day they came back again. It had been three years since she had first seen R. He was a mess — he had dropped out of engineering college, been subjected to electric shocks and his condition had worsened. He had started getting violent and had been told by a senior doctor that this was it; he would not get better and should give up on his dreams. Yet his mother remembered how Ruksheeda had said he could get better and so they were back, a third time. A glimmer of hope is all they had.

This time she did not want to take any chances, so she made them promise that they would wait till she completed her treatment before consulting another doctor. They accepted it but R didn't even look up this time. Not only was she infuriated with the doctor who had done this to him, the drawback in his condition made her task tougher. The emotional and financial strain was telling on the family as well. She knew she had to make this work for all of them.

Thus began the uphill task that looked like it was never going to end. There were more bad days than good ones. He had to be cajoled like a child. Goodies ranging from a new mobile phone to treats he loved as a child worked ... but only at times. He was sharp and would succeed in fooling his family ever so often. Only when he realised that this young doctor with all her charm was a tough cookie, did he give in to her demands with some grudging admiration. Slowly over a period of time, they became friends.

She made exceptions and took his calls sometimes even at four in the morning. She even watched National Geographic to be able to have more in common to talk about. She continued her treatment by hand-holding him, even messaging him on his mobile on his first day back in college. Yet she felt that the key to him getting better was to not let him get too dependent on her. She admitted it was a tough decision to take.

Each day there was progress. He finished his engineering course. His family was ecstatic. His confidence improved and he went alone and got admission in a premier business school.

Ruksheeda met the principal and explained how he would probably not have the best attendance but he would cope. They were supportive. Of course he was conscious of the fact that he was seven years older than his classmates. Yet he put in his best, and finally came the day that R graduated from business school, a confident man with a sterling career awaiting him.

My friend had tears in her eyes as she told me this and so did I. I congratulated her and she looked surprised. She claimed it was a team effort. Including the doctor who had demoralised him? I asked.

'He had his way and I have mine,' she smiled.

Shifa Maitra

12

KEEPING HOPE ALIVE

Only one rule in medical ethics need concern you — that action on your part which best conserves the interests of your patient.

—Martin H. Fischer

A Doctor Bows Down

When I was in the Navy, stationed as an intern on the high seas, I was witness to an amazing incident. A poor couple who worked as ship hands were expecting their first child after many years of despair. They were ecstatic when I gave them the good news. Through the naval war drills and the sirens, I could see the hope in their eyes. In between attending wounded soldiers and counseling those in recovery, the promise of their future kept us going.

Days passed, the woman went into labour, and the crew, the doctors and the naval regiment all waited with bated breath. Five hours later, she gave birth to a baby boy. He became the apple of everyone's eye; and all vied to play with him and hold him whenever they had a moment or two to spare. After a few weeks, I gradually realised that things didn't appear normal with the baby, and I didn't like what I saw.

When the ship docked, I went ashore and got all sorts of reference books. Before long I had figured out that the baby was ailing from acquired bone disease, a potentially fatal disorder. From then on, there were several consultations and treatment sessions with various doctors whenever the ship docked.

No matter what the doctor's prognosis was, the parents never lost hope. They would spend as much time as they could with the baby and would constantly pray for their son. Nothing could have been more painful than to see an ailing infant suffering mutely; especially for me, being the doctor who had helped deliver the baby. It had also been my first real experience of being an intern.

Every evening, the mother would light a lamp and pray to God to help her child recover. Soon, the symptoms became more and more apparent and I, as a doctor, scoured all the medical journals and literally began to question science. With every passing day, his movements became painfully difficult and the atmosphere on the ship became dismal, to say the least. The prospect of losing the baby seemed unbearable. Even wounded recruits found their injuries trivial in comparison.

The faith and endurance of the parents seemed to increase manifold with each passing day, which left us bewildered and awed. In the meanwhile, we tried to keep the child's pain away by administering painkillers, but there wasn't much else to do, which added to my frustration as a doctor who had just embarked on a medical career. As days passed the baby grew bigger, blissfully unaware of the fate in store for him. At two years, he could barely crawl and his limbs seemed to be slightly deformed, making it difficult for him to hold up his weight.

Then one day, I saw him holding himself up against a railing! It was a miraculous sight indeed. His blood counts showed that his platelets were increasing and though it was still short of the optimum, it was an excellent sign of recovery. His limbs seemed to be gradually straightening and I was completely overwhelmed the day I saw him taking his first steps. It was dawning on me slowly that the child was steadily recovering.

We re-started our efforts of visiting specialists, doctors and temples at every port. I turned medical journals inside out in the hope of an explanation; there was none, and I had to bow down. I was in the midst of witnessing the unfolding of a phenomenon that defied all research being done on that disease. Science may be a perfect discipline with logical explanations, and I may be in the profession of saving people, but there are still some things in the world that even a doctor cannot do that stoic belief in God can.

As told to Shashi Agarwal

Doctor Joshi

The disease was spreading its wings;
My legs, hands and wrists,
None of them had any zing.
My joints, lifeless and unkind,
Refused to obey my mind...

'Rheumatoid Arthritis,'
The diagnosis said;
Oh, the pain! I did not know how to cope;
And I was ready to give up all hope!

I reached Dr Joshi with a dismal mind;
Destiny had been terribly unkind:
I did not know what to do or say,
When I met Dr Joshi that day!

With poise and a calm demeanour,
He patiently listened to me
As my anxieties began to pour ...

Dr Joshi made me believe,
That I still had hope;
He made me see
The ways in which I could cope ...
Such a busy doctor was he;
But he had enough time for me!

He advised medicines,
And also prescribed optimism;
He stipulated fervour for life,
And recommended enthusiasm!
By the end of the day, he made it seem
I could do it, and follow my dreams.

Back into my routine
I decided to change my thinking;
Medicines did their duty,
Positivity brought back my zing!
I learnt to smile, I learnt to gleam;
Thanks to the churner of my dreams!

He kept my hope alive,
Restored my lost belief;
My life returned to normalcy,
Oh! It was such a big relief!
I thank you Dr Joshi,
For giving me a new life!

Neelam Chandra

Faith — I Take a Bow!

I met Dr K by chance while doing an article related to World No-Tobacco Day. The article was quite well appreciated and Somehow we clicked, and there began a friendship. He's an oncologist, a surgeon, and always short on time, but I gained a lot from my interactions with him. I went on to do many other articles on health and he always gave me lot of information and data to back up my arguments. I would tease him, 'It's always nice to have a doctor as a friend and guide but certainly not as his patient.'

In November 2008, my mother was diagnosed with multiple myeloma (actress Lisa Ray was diagnosed with the same and now thanks to successful stem-cell therapy, she's doing fine). To be honest, before that I was not aware of the complications associated with multiple myeloma and lots of reading on the subject made me aware of the gravity of the situation. When life gives you something difficult, it also gives you the only option of dealing with it. So, too, in our case.

I was in Orissa on a break when we first received my mother's report. The initial reaction was 'why us?' It was a feeling of shock, anger and devastation. But then we had to pick up the threads of life and move on to the next course of action. My mom's doctor looked at the report and said, 'We are sitting on a time bomb. We have to start treatment as soon as possible.' Even as the treatments started, Mom developed severe problems with her bowel movements, one of the many side-effects.

One particular day, I was all alone at home when Mom started to again feel quite bad. Her doctor was out of station so there was no way we could contact him. I wanted my mother to feel better and out of desperation, I made a call to Dr K in Ahmedabad without even thinking whether it was the right time to call him (I was always careful about not making frequent calls to doctors on their mobiles). He picked up the phone and I explained to him about the situation. He listened to me and then advised me to go to the chemist immediately, and said he would speak to the person there. Even though the medicine he prescribed was an over-the-counter one, he wanted to talk to the pharmacist.

I ran to the pharmacy in my neighbourhood, and Dr K, true to his word, called on my mobile and had a talk with the man there. After that I bought the medicine and gave it to Mom. Her problem was resolved almost instantly; nothing was more gratifying than seeing her feeling happy and relaxed.

But the story doesn't end there. It's the beginning of another story of faith — my mother instantly connected with Dr K even though she had never exchanged a word with him even over the phone, forget about meeting him. Her faith in him was absolute and complete. When I returned to Ahmedabad to rejoin work, I brought my mom's complete report with me at her insistence that 'you must show it to your doctor'.

They say faith has no logic, no rationality. There's no need to question one's faith. Many months have passed since that cruel November. Even now, there are many tough days for my mother, many difficult phases throughout her treatment. My mom always asks me one question without fail, 'Did you talk to your doctor?' And to pep her up, I tell her, 'Don't worry, I just had a talk with my doctor. He says you will be fine. This is just a passing phase because of all the treatments you have had.' That cheers her up, making her feel better instantly.

What wonders a patient's faith in a doctor can do! Even without ever meeting him, my mom has immense faith in this unseen doctor, which is much more powerful than any medicine in the world.

Deepika

A Doctor's Dream

Sitting in a dimly lit area outside a courtroom, a certain
doctor comes to my mind,
A smile spreads across my face; he was definitely one of a
kind.
I remember the packed J.J. Hospital auditorium waiting for
his lecture to begin,
His thoughts and extensive knowledge made sure the words
sunk right in.

Even while taking oral exams he'd teach more than question,
He welcomed both doubts and suggestions.
Even as a student his seniors called him to deliver spinal
taps,
His queries made the best of doctors put on their thinking
caps.

When he passed by, the nurses whispered about his skills
and dedication,

Of his generosity and attention towards patients of any caste
and vocation,
His colleagues lauded his great ability to diagnose and his
judgement sound,
No patient ever feared death when this doctor was around.

He got many offers to go abroad for a better life,
But he chose to remain in India and for the patients strive.
Time had no meaning; he worked around the clock,
It never occurred to him that this was causing a heart block.

A renowned doctor, he wanted to save lives with all his
might,
He saw at the dark end of every tunnel, a beam of pure
white light.
He built a hospital with new machines and first class health
care,
In the process he kept ignoring his own health scares.

His little girl once put up a 'Take it easy' sign
But the hospital, his patients, were the only things on his
mind
Day and night he toiled for patients both rich and poor,
As he found ways to treat diseases, he opened new doors.

As is the way of the world, a legal dispute arose over the
hospital land,
The money he had earned was flowing away from his hand.
It was not the loss of money that disturbed him; it was the
loss of people's hope,

Seeing despair in their eyes was something with which he
could not cope.
He fought for his rights and for the lives of patients too,
But no one other than paid attorneys heard his voice, which
was growing older too.

One night his little daughter ran scared, into his arms,
'Baby girl, I'm right here. Nothing will happen to you, you
are safe from harm.'
'No Daddy,' said the girl, 'It isn't me I'm worried about, it is
you who seem to be fading away,
You need rest Daddy, let us go out for a day.'

He did not rest; for he did not have the time,
He was a doctor and for the sake of the hospital he was
prepared to run millions of miles.
The fact that his heart was not keeping up did not trouble
him at all,
A little chest pain was not going to stop him from standing
tall.

The hospital and the courtroom, his schedule revolved
around them all the time,
Going home and sleeping peacefully now seemed like a
crime.
Neither his wife nor his son nor his daughter brought him
any peace,
Even at home he seemed always ill at ease.

He was cheated of his hospital land and was fighting harder than ever,
He could not let his patients down, he would do that never.
Then one night his magnanimous heart finally gave away,
He took one last look at the match on the television before he began to sway.

Neither his son who was a medical student, nor his eighth grade daughter
Nor his gynaecologist wife could save his life,
It seemed the doctor had been dealt with an overdose of strife.
The doctor's dreams, his work and his aspirations all seemed to be in vain,
He would now never be able to return again.

'Case No. 4321, Dr Verma versus Aslam Ali,' the court scribe shouted out,
I went in, the way I had for more than two years now.
'And who are you?' the new judge gruffly asked,
'I am Priyadarshini Verma, Dr Verma's daughter,' said I.
'I've been coming to get justice for the father who is no longer here,
His dedication, compassion and morality make him, in my mind, so very dear!'

Rajivi Prabhakar Rao

Never Give Up

She was pale, clammy and gasping for breath. It appeared to us, the medical team, that God was calling her. Her parents were looking at her with pain, disbelief, anxiety, worry and as they looked into our eyes, all this turned into hope.

Her heart was not functioning properly, it was not pumping. Her condition was called dilated cardiomyopathy in medical terminology. They reported that she had been a healthy ten-year-old until a week ago when she became progressively breathless until she reached this stage. Can you imagine the pain of a family to see a bubbly healthy child reach the precipice of death so suddenly?

The consultant in charge looked at the little girl and said, 'It's too late, there is no point trying.' I was the junior doctor on duty during this episode. I looked into her eyes and saw courage, the ability to fight and faith in us, the medical team. I mentally decided that I would do everything in my power to save her.

But what could one do when the heart was not pumping properly? Her heart rate was at a steady two hundred, and her blood reports had come back okay. I started her on the standard medications that we do in these situations ... but there was no response. Behind the oxygen mask her desperate face was impossible to watch. I stayed at her bedside, a junior doctor trying everything she knew, but realising that medical science has its limitations.

Eight hours later, something suddenly struck me — her heart rate was still a steady two hundred, could it be she had tachycardia-induced cardiomyopathy, a condition where a fast heart rate leads to the heart not functioning, but a treatable situation. Could it be?

It was 1 a.m., the senior consultant was at home and I had no one to ask if this was a possibility. We had nothing to lose, she was going down rapidly. That night, I took my chances and started two medications for arrhythmias — digoxin and amiodarone; the second one could be dangerous if I was not right, and life-saving, if I was.

The whole night I monitored her, administered the treatment, and sat at her bedside until my eyes could stay open no longer. At seven the next morning, something magical happened. The medications had worked — the heart rate slowed to 140/minute, her heart started working again, the colour returned to her face and for the time being her condition seemed to have improved. I had taken a chance and it had worked.

She looked up at me from behind the oxygen mask and the lines and the tubes and whispered so softly that I could barely hear her: 'Thank you, Doctor.' That night taught me something invaluable — to never give up on a patient and to never stop thinking about alternatives. Never give up on life. Never give up.

Dr Sunita Maheshwari

Restoring Faith

I was on ICU rotation duty during my internal medicine residency. Most of the patients I attended to were comatose or too ill to communicate. I was getting used to the silence and the humming of the machines, when Arun was admitted to the ICU.

He was a stout gentleman, around fifty years of age, with a perpetual smile on his face. My maiden name was Aruna and it seemed like we had an instant connection. He was admitted for ascites (accumulation of fluids in the abdominal cavity). As I secured an intravenous line for fluid support and antibiotics for him, he started talking to me. He spoke cheerfully, telling me that he was an alcoholic and kept on repeating a line from some old movie, 'Sharaab pine se liver kharab hota hai' (alcohol damages the liver). I liked him instantly.

He stayed for more than a month, which gave us a long time to interact. He used to wait for my visits and I started looking forward to meeting him. He would talk a lot about himself and his stories revolved around his children, his wife and alcohol.

One day a colleague called me up and requested me to rush

to the ICU. I went there only to find that she was trying to secure an IV line for Arun and since she could not find a patent vein, she had done a venesection (a skin incision to introduce the catheter into the vein). She had already made a big cut on the skin of his leg and was still not able to see any vein. Arun was bleeding profusely. She begged me to finish the procedure; I was no expert myself, and realised that we had a messy situation here.

I was anxious and alarmed. I looked at Arun, who appeared calm despite the excruciating pain. He had a strange look of peace on his face in spite of knowing that we had goofed up. I felt guilty but his patience and composure reassured me. I widened the incision and located a vein. By the time we had completed the procedure, we knew that we had made an extra large opening where a small nick would have sufficed. The effect of the local anaesthesia had long worn off. Arun was definitely in a lot of pain. After I had finished he said, 'I am sure you have done the best venesection ever. Don't worry; I'm going to be just fine.' He was comforting me instead of it being the other way round.

After this incident, I started visiting him even more frequently just to ensure that all was well with him. But he developed hepatorenal syndrome, a rare but deadly complication of ascites related to cirrhosis of the liver and which leads to kidney failure. After a few days he contracted congestive heart failure and during one of my visits, I looked at him to realise that he had gone into cardiac arrest!

All I could think of was to give him a DC shock using a defibrillator as a final measure. I was almost in a trance-like state when I administered the shock, recalling every second that I had spent with him. I prayed to God to show his magical powers and revive him. I knew of the defibrillator as a device that could quickly produce dramatic improvements in a patient's health. Having seen it being used only in movies, I always thought that its function was exaggerated.

Yet, I tried again, this time more vigorously. I could see some muscle contraction and changes in his flat ECG line — Arun had come back to life. He was alive. After he regained consciousness, his first words were, 'Hey Doc, I knew you would get me back.'

Arun lived for three weeks after that, which was more than anyone had hoped for. But this incident stays engraved in my memory forever. I realised that the trust a patient bestows on a doctor can be so powerful that it can change the entire concept of medicine.

Every patient I treat reminds me of Arun and every judgment I make, is with the thought of retaining the faith of the patient.

Rugvedita Parakh

The Book

The world collapsed around me when my mother called with the news that my father had suffered a severe cerebral haemorrhage. My parents were in good health and apart from the occasional visit to the general practitioner, our interactions with the medical community had been minimal. It was difficult for me to accept that my father, my hero, the man who could do everything from fixing a car to cooking the yummiest dishes to in the world, was on a hospital bed, fighting for his life.

It was twenty-four hours before I finally saw my father in the ICU. His smile was intact; I was so relieved. The doctors said that he had lost the use of his right limbs and speech but it was not irreversible. But, as fate would have it, within the span of a few hours my father slipped into a coma.

My husband's doctor put us onto the best neurosurgeon in town, Dr Sanjay Kumar, who agreed to meet me at very short notice on a Sunday. Dr Kumar was a well-known doctor in the community and had the reputation of being a miracle worker. My hopes were riding high when I met him, but his prognosis was disheartening. He said, 'A hundred percent victory would be to take your father home, alive.' His words broke my heart but then he went on to explain the delicacy of the situation and the unpredictability of recovery.

We moved my father to Apollo Hospital under the care of Dr Kumar, where he was kept in an isolated ward in the MICU. The other doctors were not very confident that he would pull through, but Dr Kumar was unwilling to give up. He put together the best team to monitor my father. I noticed the doctors talking to my father even when he was in a coma; this really gave me hope and made my belief in their dedication even stronger.

Days turned to weeks; my routine and his recovery status remained unchanged. Every morning I used to take the first bus to the hospital, spend the day sitting outside the ICU and return on the last bus to town. I used to carry a book with me to avoid conversation with other family members of patients in the ICU. I didn't want to talk to them; I didn't want to know who they were praying for. Dr Kumar noticed my mechanical demeanour and saw it as early signs of depression (as he later told me).

'Let me keep this for the day,' he surprised me by asking me for my book, one morning. I hesitated for a moment and then obeyed without any questions. I was upset. Now I had nothing to preoccupy me.

'It will be impossible to pull through the day!' I grumbled. After fifteen minutes of silence, I got talking to the others who had been waiting outside the ICU for the last few days. I met the mother of a young jawan who had lost his legs in a mine blast. I spoke at length with a young mother of two whose husband's kidneys were failing. I made friends with the mother of a two-year-old who had fallen from their first floor house and cracked his skull. I realised that everybody had their own miseries and as we shared our sorrows, I felt better and stronger. I realised why Dr Kumar had taken away my book.

I watched the doctors deal with broken bones, bruised egos and scared patients with equal commitment and patience, and as the days went by I befriended the doctors and the nurses. They had several stories to tell us — miracles they had seen, courage that made them cry, and most of all the unfailing trust that they seemed to evoke in all.

One day when we were in one of those gloomy moods, Dr Kumar narrated an incident to us. One of his patients, a young girl, had been through a brain surgery and was recovering well. She was ready to be discharged and the doctor gave the parents a list of do's and don'ts to follow. One of his instructions was that the mother should give a bath to the girl after a week. When the girl and her parents met the doctor after a month, the girl complained of boils and rashes all over her body. The parents had assumed that it was a side-effect of some medication, but the doctor refused to accept this probability. On detailed consultation, the doctor realised that the girl had not been bathed at all during the month except for that one time, a week from the day of release, since the doctor had said 'give a bath after a week'! We laughed heartily, forgetting our grief for a few moments as Dr Kumar walked away with a grin.

It was almost as if Dr Kumar and his team had taken it upon themselves to not just focus on the patients, our loved ones, but at the same time to keep us going too. Their smiles and stories kept me sane in a hopeless environment.

My father subsequently came out of his coma and a month later we brought him back home. Today, two long years later, he can wobble and walk, can pronounce certain words and is responsive to the environment. The doctors call it a miracle and they have helped me believe that I can still hope for the day I will be able to hold his arm and walk down the road.

Amrita Srinivasan

The Dream

A few years ago I was working for a reputed NGO, and my job required me to visit a hospital and spend time with terminally-ill patients, who didn't have very much time. I used to sit with the patients, crack jokes, sing and read to them. It was rewarding to see a smile on their faces, even for a few moments.

The doctors and nurses were helpful and sensitive. However, there was one particular doctor, Dr Umang, who was always in great demand, but very irregular. There was always a crowd of patients waiting for him as he was the leading cardiologist in that hospital. Someone told me that he was working elsewhere for additional income, as the government salary was not enough for him. He was obviously an ambitious man. Watching people wait patiently for long hours irritated me, and I thought money was more important to him than the well-being of his patients.

A few months passed and I got busy with other assignments. One day when I returned home from work, my mother handed me an envelope. I opened it — it was an invitation card from

Dr Umang for the opening of his new charitable hospital for heart disease and cancer care. The card read: 'Please come and visit my dream hospital.'

The hospital was named after his mother. It was vast and well planned, with all the latest equipment and free treatment for the underprivileged. Dr Umang's mother had died of cancer, and at that time his family did not have enough money to save her. Today he was a leading cardiologist and wanted the deprived and the needy to come to his hospital for treatment, without any worries and hesitation.

It was then that I figured out the reason behind the doctor's irregularity at the government hospital. He had been busy building his dream project that would improve the lives of so many. I felt guilty for being hasty in forming an opinion about him. Sometimes what we observe is not always true; what we do for ourselves dies with us, but what we do for others remains.

Dr Umang will be always remembered, for his magnanimous contribution to society, in the form of the hospital.

Aparna Mathur

13

ON GRATITUDE

Gratitude is the memory of the heart.
—Jean Baptiste Massieu

A Chapati of Jowar

I was driving to work, gazing out of my window, when I caught sight of a blind woman scouring a garbage lot near some shacks at a construction site.

I stopped my car, took a U-turn and reached the site.

I went to her though I was sure that I would be met with hostility from her and the other women-folk around her. I started a general conversation with her, asked about her work, how long had they lived in that place, her kids, etc. Then, I gently asked her, 'Can you see well?'

After spending a good half an hour with them, I told her that I was an ophthalmologist and could help her see again. I felt that she was afflicted with optic neuritis (a visually threatening disease) in both eyes. I had treated such patients before.

She gazed into the distance and thought about it for sometime, then said, 'No ... I don't wish to be treated ...'

I was taken aback, but being a mother myself, I could guess her thoughts.... She was thinking about her children, aged two and four years respectively, and that there would be nobody to take care of them while was gone for her treatment.

A voice in me said, 'Do not leave this patient alone.'

And then the zeal of the doctor, the tenderness of a mother and the compassion of a human being took over me.

I said, 'I have a great idea, let me take you and your kids to my clinic in my car and while I examine and treat you, your kids can have a meal and play with toys.'

She agreed and asked another lady to accompany them. So, in my car, accompanied by her two children and friend, she started her journey of hope.

As I had thought, she had acutely inflamed optic nerves in both eyes. I treated her with intravenous doses of a strong medicine on the first day, with her kids around her enjoying their meal and playing with toys.

After the first day's treatment was over, I dropped her off near her locality but with a promise that she had to follow this ritual every day for about a week.

Her vision started improving from the next day itself. On the second day, all of them were waiting for me when my car stopped. She hugged me, bowed a little, her eyes brimming with tears. She then silently hopped into my car, and we drove off; she had developed a sense of security with me as her vision improved. This ritual went on for about ten days and by God's grace she was cured of her illness.

On the last day of the treatment, I asked her why she had refused treatment the first time. She said, 'Who would have looked after my kids if I took care of myself?'

I was touched that, in spite of the fact that she was going blind, she had thought about her children first. On the fifteenth day, I passed by the site one morning and found the place deserted. I inquired with the watchman and he said that the labourers had left the site, but the woman, Sita, had left something in a newspaper for me — a chapati of jowar. I understood that it had been wrapped up with her joy at being able to see again — and of course, her love and gratitude.

Tears welled up in my eyes. It's rightly said, 'Some people come into our lives for a reason.' Destiny had chosen us to meet, do our bit and depart even without bidding goodbye. It's been two years now and I have not seen her again but I pray and wish her well always.

I pray to God to retain in me the zeal of a doctor and the compassion of a human being.

Neebha Haribhakti

Change

For the first fifteen years of my life, I lived in places you've probably never heard of — Mhow, Abohar, Fazilka, Bambolim and Chandimandir — all military cantonments. Medical problems meant dashing to the MI room, where the nurse on duty would apply a tincture, or give you some tonic or white pills to swallow. In all those years, what I never saw was a chemist's shop.

But as the old cliché goes, the only constant in life is change. Dad retired and we transitioned to civilian life. We were thrust right into the hustle and bustle of Mumbai, and that was the end of the languid cantonment atmosphere. The second change came with the doctors.

Now I was going to some converted shop that doubled as a 'clinic'. There would be all kinds of people waiting before me — old men anxious to talk about their ailments, bawling babies in the arms of their mothers, children keen on destroying garish vases with plastic flowers, old women in ghunghats who ensured one foot space on either side on the bench they were

sitting on. Then I would go in and see the doctor who would
dismiss me in five minutes flat. He would use his stethoscope,
jam a thermometer between my teeth, shine a torch down my
throat, write a prescription, thrust it hurriedly in my hands
and press the bell for 'next'.

When the 'civilian' doctor had pushed me out, I would head
off to a chemist's shop and discover that one actually had to
pay for medicines. Who knew a strip of tiny white pills could
cost more than a week's groceries?

And I would have to go back again and again, because
the ailment either never went away completely, or had
developed complications. I contracted all kinds of diseases in
my first few months in Mumbai — dysentery, eye infections,
backaches (due to travelling in the local trains), rashes …
the list could just go on.

And then Dr More happened.

We moved to a colony in Thane, and right below our flat was
Dr More's clinic. Three days into that house and I had my first
visit scheduled for the doctor.

There was hardly anyone in the clinic, which was a bit
surprising. Mumbai clinics are never so empty. The assistant
was busy cleaning the floor and doing other chores. After
some time a pleasant gentleman walked in. I thought he
was the doctor, but the assistant quite snappily put him in
his place. That happened to the next three gentlemen until
a middle-aged, short, bald man walked in. The assistant's
behaviour now changed to deference, and I realised he was
the doctor. He didn't seem to have the gruff 'I'm-too-busy-
to-answer-your-pesky-questions' attitude that I had seen in
other doctors.

I went in and started talking about my physical problems.
He poked my torso with his stethoscope (I've never liked
the procedure, because I'm ticklish). Then he asked me
many questions, like where and what had I'd eaten, whether
I drank boiled water, etc. He then went on to say that my
stomach had rebelled against the street food that I had been
consuming. He reached out to a shelf full of little jars with
pills in almost all colours.

I received three magenta pills to be taken for a day after
meals, two turquoise pills for morning and night, and one small
white pill for emergency, if I had dysentery. He counted out the
pills for three days, put them in a tiny plastic self-locking bag,
told me to pay the compounder twenty rupees, and wished me
a good day with a bright smile.

Whoever had heard of a doctor like that? What were in those
pills, by the way? Why didn't he write a prescription? I could at
least look up the drug names on the Internet instead of staying
awake all night worrying about side-effects.

Since I couldn't do better, and was in no mood for a second
opinion, I swallowed those pills as instructed. Next morning,
to my amazement, I was fine and fit as a fiddle.

When I went to him for the next ailment, I got green,
yellow and pink pills. My complaint disappeared the next
morning. For the next disorder I got grey and pink mosaic
pills. And voila! The problem vanished by morning. Was
there any drug in them at all, or was it just the doctor's
pleasant ways? I've never ever met a doctor like him in
my life.

Even today, fifteen years later, we rush to him for every
little sickness and all it takes is one dose of his coloured and

nameless pills to do the trick. And we haven't seen a chemist's shop in all these years.

Sometimes, change is nice. And sometimes, it's nice to have things the way they were, like Dr More and his pills. Thank you for no change, Dr More.

Raamesh Gowri Raghavan

Colours of Darkness

'Water ... give me some water, Doctor,' she cried. 'I hate green chillies!' she complained wiping her nose.

'It's not chillies; it's green ... from now on chillies stands for the colour green, Appu.'

Apsara or Appu had been my classmate since the fifth grade. She was amazingly gifted as an artist and won all the painting competitions held in school. Her brush created magic on the canvas. While all of us were feeling pressurised by the looming board exams, Appu was looking forward to a painting competition to be held in April after the exams. Winning this competition would be a dream come true for her as the winning piece would be exhibited all over the country. It would be put up for auction as well. For a fifteen-year-old, it would be a huge achievement.

It was Diwali time that year. The last thing Appu saw from her car window was a dazzling firecracker that burst into the sky spreading colorful sparkles all over. And then ...there was darkness. Their car had collided with a truck on their way back home from Appu's aunt's place.

Two days after the accident Appu opened her eyes to absolute darkness. She had lost her vision, but only temporarily, as the doctors explained. With appropriate treatment and a surgery, Appu would get her vision back. The operation would be performed after ten months as that was the time she needed to recuperate from the other internal injuries and loss of blood.

Appu would lose one academic year but it didn't matter. Her family was more than grateful that she was safe. But Appu was shattered; after a lot of hard work she had been selected as a finalist in the national painting competition but her dreams had come crashing down.

'Tears are saline water. They aren't good for your eyes, Apsara. You will be all right. This darkness is just temporary,' Dr Rushdie consoled her.

'No, Doctor. This darkness is here to stay.'

Dr Rushdie was an eye-specialist, but he was well aware of the misery his patients experienced while fighting such tragic situations in their lives.

'You are too young to bow down to the ruthless blows of destiny, my child. Your life is yet to begin. You have to learn to fight.'

'How do I fight, Doctor?'

'Appu, we have five senses. You have lost just one of them. But you can still make use of the other four senses to fulfil your dream.'

Dr Rushdie then bought painting material for Appu. He had given a distinct scent to each color so that Appu could relate to them. Green paint smelt like crushed green chilies, red had the aroma of tomatoes, pink smelt like rose, blue had the fragrance of deodorant, and black was like black currants.

Initially, it all seemed too tough, but the doctor and his patient spent hours together to make things happen. After learning to recognise colours by smell, Dr Rushdie taught her how to measure the canvas with her fingers, to make out the position of her strokes. After months of painstaking practice, Appu finally aced the art of painting without vision.

The jury was spellbound by her paintings. No one could believe that the artist of such spectacular work was visually impaired. Appu wasn't the winner but her work was chosen to be exhibited and eventually auctioned.

By the end of the year, Appu regained her eyesight after a successful surgery, just in time to attend the auction. The bid for her painting went up to four lakhs rupees! But the young fifteen-year-old artist rejected the offer.

'This painting is called "Colours of Darkness" and is dedicated to the man who showed me how to create colours even in obscurity,' she announced. 'This is my gift to my mentor, my doctor, Dr Rushdie.'

'Hey Doctor, don't cry! You are growing old. Tears are saline water and they aren't good for your eyes,' said Apsara to the sixty-eight-year-old eye-specialist who couldn't control his tears when his young patient gifted him with what would be the most priceless possession of her life.

Avantika Debnath

Crossroads

Sleep was fitful and Ajay dreamt of ECG machines. Night duty was tough. He got up and decided to walk to Mundoos for a cup of masala chai. Mundoos was run by a Nepali boy, who used to work in one of the nearby homes until he decided to put his skills to more profitable use. Not that his culinary skills were anythng to boast of, but he certainly knew how to brew a good tea. The doctor's fetish for tea kept him busy and in business.

'Looks like you had a bad night, Doctor Sahib,' Mundoo grinned, and quickly set about preparing some fresh tea. Ajay sat on a wooden bench facing the road that led to the railway station. Even at 7 a.m. on a chilly winter morning, scooters and auto rickshaws buzzed past.

'So, Doctor Sahib, did you manage to catch *Big Boss* yesterday night?' He crushed some cloves and green cardamoms with a wooden rolling pin and tossed them into a black pan. Ajay shook his head and waited for Mundoo to launch forth on last night's episode. It was funny how the uniting factor amongst people was greed and voyeurism, as the reality shows had demonstrated.

Ajay knew he could not go on like this for long. He had to strike it big somehow.... He cradled the tea glass in his hands and held it close to his face, letting the vapours suffuse his cold cheeks. He could not see himself spending his years walking down the corridors of Mission Hospital, a venerable but decaying institution; treating patients with equipment that barely functioned, prescribing medicines that were not available because somebody had siphoned them off, witnessing the abject poverty of his patients, and the misery that engulfed them when they realised the prohibitive cost of treatment. His salary was a pittance; there was no way one could live well in his meagre monthly stipend.

The circumstances under which they functioned in the small town were deplorable. Just recently the power had gone off when he was assisting in an operation, and the generator was out of order. There lay the patient on the operating table, his abdomen cut open, doctors in masks and gloves, holding implements, hovering dubiously in the sudden dark. A resourceful nurse had fetched an emergency light from the nearest chemist store and they had managed to somehow perform the surgery.

There were other sources of income for most employees of the hospital. His colleagues sniggered that he didn't know how, but of course he knew. He liked the good life but wanted to earn money honourably.

'What an irony!' he thought. As a doctor your job is to put people out of their suffering, and here, the profession thrived on others' misery. He knew if he stayed long enough, the system would suck him in — innocuously, at first ....

A week earlier an elderly woman had walked in with her

husband into the OPD (Out Patient Department). The woman was suffering from recurrent headaches, and some blurring of vision. The husband was visibly concerned and suspected something serious. Ajay knew a CT scan was needed to enable a correct diagnosis. A referral to one of the private diagnostic clinics meant a twenty per cent commission for the doctor, and that was a lot. He could easily double his monthly internship stipend ....

He had almost given in to the temptation when he happened to notice the woman's chadar. It was patched and had frayed edges. Ajay felt remorse and shame at his weakness, and quickly signed a referral to the local government hospital. The incident had stayed with him though, mocking him.

***

It had been a long and tiring thirty-six hours. After attending to his last patient for the day, Ajay collected his keys and walked out of the OPD room. He was looking forward to the warm dinner at home with his mother — something that added cheer to his bleak routine. As he turned the corner to step into the parking lot, he heard somebody call out loudly, 'Doctor Sahib!'

Ajay turned back to see a familiar face. 'We got the scan done, as you had suggested,' said the husband of the woman with the frayed chadar.

'Good,' he said. 'Come tomorrow with the reports and we will discuss the case.' He started to move towards the parking lot.

'I will, Doctor Sahib. I ... I just wanted you to know how grateful we are to you for your thoughtfulness. We know now that we are in good hands.' Ajay stopped and looked at the old man weeping tears of gratitude.

The blessing and good wishes coming from the old man worked like a balm, soothing all the exasperation caused by his dilemma. As Ajay kicked his scooter to life, and rode off, he thanked God for helping him not to give in to temptations that may make him a rich man but would take away his peace of mind forever.

Manreet Sodhi Someshwar

In the Best Hands

Nanavati Hospital, Mumbai, Paediatric ward, 2.40 a.m.

'Ma'am, please switch off the nebuliser, once the medicine in it finishes,' said the nurse to a very tired but sleepless me. As she was walking out of the room, she turned around, looked at me and said, 'Ma'am, please try and get some sleep.' I nodded and smiled at her concern.

Just a few hours ago, Maanya, my daughter, had complained of a mild chest pain, which was a complication arising from an asthmatic attack. Our doctor, Dr Ninad, had wound up for the day, but I had called him up and explained the situation. Without any hesitation he asked me to bring Maanya over to his home for a check-up. By now, Maanya was in a lot of discomfort, and the agony of seeing my child in that state was reflected on my face. We had barely entered Ninad's home when Maanya threw up. Ninad was very calm. He urged me to relax, and began to check Maanya's pulse and her breathing. I knew that Maanya was not in a very good state and I was sure the doctor saw that too. Very, very calmly he made a few calls and told us to admit Maanya in Nanavati Hospital. He made sure that all necessary arrangements were made before we reached the hospital.

At about 11 p.m., we were watching Maanya sleep when Ninad walked in. He checked up on Maanya and smiled. He then looked at me and said reassuringly, 'Your girl is much stronger and braver than you are, Vandana. Just look at her, one dose of medication and she is better already. Why do you worry so much? I am always here for your girl.'

The next morning, 7 a.m.

The breakfast arrives, I'm still asleep. I hear Maanya calling out to me. I wake up to see my baby looking so much better, the colour back in her cheeks and she is eagerly looking at the upma on the breakfast tray.

The two- hourly nebulisation continued, and at around 9.30 a.m., we were visited by a doctor who was presumably on the hospital panel. He went through Maanya's papers and talked to the nurse about the course of treatment. I began to tell him a few things I thought were important and that he have knowledge of, but he cut me off abruptly and said he did not need those details.

I kept quiet and waited for Ninad to show up. He didn't.

I tried to call him a number of times during the day, but his cell phone was switched off. We didn't see our doctor the whole day and that made me very uncomfortable.

The next morning, the doctor on the panel arrived. He took a perfunctory look at Maanya's papers and left. I thought, 'Will he not check her breathing, ask me how she's been, her food intake, her general condition, etc?' But then I said to myself, 'Never mind, Vandana, Ninad will be here today and you can tell him all.'

But Ninad did not come.

Then, late in the evening, there was a knock at the door, and Ninad walked in. His head shaved completely, stubble on his face and eyes swollen. He sat on the bed with Maanya and began to chat with her, all the while checking her breathing with his stethoscope. He then looked at me and said, 'Maanya is ready to go home.' He was astonished at the speed of recovery that Maanya was showing.

But in my heart I know that my child received comfort from her doctor's care and that helped her get better faster than any medication ever could. We talked about why and what exactly happened to Maanya. I could see he was not his usual self. I asked him why he had not come to see Maanya the day before. He looked at me and I saw something I'd never seen in his eyes before — grief. 'I lost my mother yesterday, Vandana,' he said. 'My home is full of relatives and we have a number of rituals to be performed today, but I had to come see Maanya.'

At that moment I knew my girl was in the care of the best doctor in the world. He truly is what a doctor ought to be.

Vandana Vij

It Worked Both Ways

It was a small railway township and had its own hospital, school and other facilities.

There was a kind of fellowship, intimacy and empathy among the residents as they all worked for the same employer — the Indian Railways. It was a small community where we all knew each other; in fact it was like one big, happy family. So our speech was often interspersed with a lot of 'our teachers', 'our doctors', 'our hospital'.

I cannot help remembering with a smile that even the trains were given names. One could often hear people saying, '101 (the train number) is running an hour late, and "he" will not be here before two o' clock'!

Our family was a part of the above scenario. We did not think twice before requesting our doctor for a house visit when the need arose nor did the doctor feel that he was doing us a big favour and put on airs.

I was about twelve years old then and a chronic asthma patient. Any change in the weather meant an attack!

Once, as usual, I suffered a severe asthmatic attack when the weather turned nasty and I was so unwell that I was not fit to be taken to the hospital.

My father requested the doctor on duty to come home to attend to me. Dr Srivatsan promised to come after his evening rounds at the hospital. He was a new doctor and had recently come on a transfer to our town.

It was eight at night when the doctor started off for our home. It was raining heavily, and the doctor, who was on his cycle, was caught off guard. He did not have a rain coat and to add to his woes, he was not familiar with the town and had to search for our house. Under these difficult circumstances, he could have easily gone back postponing his visit to the morning, but to his credit he did not do that.

By the time he reached our home, he was fully drenched. My parents tried their best to reduce his discomfort. Though he accepted a cup of coffee and a towel to dry his hair, he refused to change into dry clothes offered by my father. He attended to me, gave me an injection to bring down the severity of the attack, prescribed some medication, sat with me for an hour to see that I was comfortable and only then left as the rain began to stop.

The next morning my father went to the hospital to report to the doctor, but he learnt that the doctor had fever and had taken a few days off. My father went to his quarters, told him that I was better and sat with him for some time before taking his leave.

But the doctor's fever refused to come down and after about fifteen days, he was diagnosed with tuberculosis. My father firmly believed that it was the doctor's visit to our place in the pouring rain that had caused him the infection and felt very guilty, however much the doctor, who had become like a friend by now, tried telling him that it was a latent condition that had been brought out by the exposure and actually the visit had done him good for it had led to the diagnosis.

My father admired Dr Srivatsan and called him a perfect gentleman and a conscientious professional. The doctor was admitted to the Tambaram Sanatorium near Chennai for isolation and treatment. His wife and aged father too shifted to Chennai to be near him. His seventeen-year-old son stayed back in the hostel attached to the college where he was studying in the Intermediate Course. The boy was studying Biology, Chemistry and Physics as he was interested in studying medicine. Dr Srivatsan was worried about his son, Vinu, as the boy had an easy-going nature and without parental guidance might not make the grade.

My father felt that he should repay the doctor's kindness in some way.

Fortunately, it so happened that my father's cousin was a lecturer and a warden in Vinu's college. My father explained to him how the boy was special and that at any cost he should do well in his studies so that he could qualify for the medical course.

My uncle paid heed to my father's request, and asked his colleagues in the respective departments to take special care with that boy. Later on, when the results were declared it was obvious that they had done exactly that.

My father used to go to Chennai on duty once every three weeks and we suspected that it was mainly to visit the doctor at the sanatorium and assure him that his son was in good hands.

Through his cousin, my father kept a close watch on Vinu's progress and the fact that Uncle was also the hostel warden helped. Vinu did not know why the warden was hounding him all the time and watching his progress like a hawk! He did not know of the warden's relationship to my father.

However, the combined efforts of the teachers and my uncle made Vinu put in the required hard work and it paid off.

Vinu passed his examination with good marks which enabled him to enter medical college. Dr Srivatsan's discharge from the sanatorium coincided with this happy event. He was declared fully cured of tuberculosis. My father sighed in relief, and said, 'My debt is settled in full measure.'

Revathi Seshadri

Some More Time

He was blue, like Lord Krishna. Every step was an effort, breathless and tired. There was not enough oxygen in this one-year-old's blood. He had been refused surgery at every hospital in India.

His parents had brought him to our hospital in Bangalore all the way from Kashmir as a last resort. After examining him we found he had a single right ventricle with pulmonary stenosis and heterotaxy — a situation where only one chamber of the heart had developed. We told them we could try and operate, but it would be a high-risk operation. There were no guarantees and we weren't sure of the long-term results of the surgery. He might not make it.

They simply said, 'Doctor, please try.'

And so we did. The team took him on. He had a catheterisation and a Glenn shunt. And by God's grace, he made it through! He was unrecognisable, having changed in a few hours from blue to pink. The family distributed sweets to all the doctors and nurses and returned up north.

Many years later, a blue four-year-old walked into my clinic. It was 'Krishna', back with his parents. He had done well for three years but he was blue and breathless again. His valve was leaking, the Glenn was not enough. He would need another operation, with even higher risk and even fewer guarantees.

'Try, Doctor,' they said.

And so we did. But this time all the miracles of modern science could not save him. His valve was fixed and a Fontan was done — a five-hour surgery. But he never made it out of the operating room. His time had come. I cried with his parents.

A year later there was a knock on the door of my clinic. No child, just his parents. They must have seen the concern on my face — it was very unusual for a family to return after their child had died. Were they coming back to sue me for his death?

But no ... they came in and touched my feet. 'It has been one year since we lost him, Doctor. It has been a very difficult year. We had bought a house when our baby was born. But after he died, we could not bear to live there any longer with all the memories. We sold the house and moved to Delhi. It is his first death anniversary today. We came to thank you for taking a chance and agreeing to operate on him the first time when every hospital had refused. We know he eventually did not make it. But you tried. And because of that we had him with us for three more years — three wonderful, magical, beautiful years. And for that we will always be grateful.'

I cried with his parents again.

Dr Sunita Maheswari

Thank you, Dr K!

I was miserable on the way back from the doctor's clinic. Tears welled up and ran down my cheeks.

'What is it?' Mom quizzed.

'It's my right ear. I don't think I hear too well,' I said, wiping the tears on my sleeve.

'Are you sure?' she asked, peeping into my ear.

'Yes! When Dr K stood on my right and explained the prescription to you, I didn't hear a word!' I wailed.

Mom couldn't control her laughter. Later on, I came to know that Dr K was the most soft-spoken person one could ever encounter and my ear had nothing to do with it! It was said that anybody who stood a foot away from the doctor couldn't hear him. As a six-year-old, I didn't know that. This incident took place almost eighteen years ago.

I grew up and transformed from a six-year-old drama queen to an ambitious young woman. After my graduation, I bagged a job in a multinational company. Thanks to the MNC culture, all the sophistication went to my head and the sedentary lifestyle didn't help my health either. I soon developed severe asthma and low blood pressure.

My mother grew concerned and continuously reminded me to go visit Dr K.

'How many more reminders do you need?' she would often rebuke me over the phone.

'Why do you insist I should only see him?' I demanded. 'I have taken an appointment at the new, modern hospital with a senior doctor. The modern hospitals are better than the small clinics any day!' I replied cockily.

'Well, your choice,' she said. The next moment, I heard a click on the other end of the phone. I had very little time to worry why Mom had hung up on me, as I had to rush for a conference call.

I went to the modern hospital the next day. 'How can I help you, Ma'am?' the receptionist asked me politely. All the pleasantries made me feel good until I got the bill — Rs 500 for registration and Rs 750 for consultation. The company's 'med-claim policy' was there to back me up so I tried not to care, but somehow it did make me think....

I went from one hospital to another as my condition worsened. All the air-conditioning and the comfortable chairs in the huge hospitals did not provide any comfort. Even after running from pillar to post, taking a cocktail of syrups and popping pills with weird names, nothing had changed. 'All that glitters is not gold,' I thought to myself and finally decided to go straight to Dr K.

I walked in and waited, with no appointment and no registration. It felt like a home-coming. I sat patiently on the wooden bench. Despite having no air-conditioning, the clinic felt cool and comfortable even on a hot summer's day. I guess the clinic reflected the aura of the man who ran it — cool, calm and simple.

As I walked into his immaculately clean chamber, I was consumed by guilt but greeted him with a smile. A man of few words, he asked me what I was suffering from. After the diagnosis, he prescribed an inhaler and handed over some free pills in a brown paper bag.

'Use the inhaler only when the wheezing is more pronounced than usual or in case of an emergency. Eat healthy, exercise and practice pranayam regularly. That should take care of it,' he said.

'Thank you,' I said. That was it. No unnecessary medicines and tests. How come the other doctors failed to keep it so simple? And he was right, it did work. It's been three years now and I'm still free from asthma.

Even when prices shot up with the booming economy, Dr K unlike others didn't increase his fee. He kept giving away free medicines depending on the availability and charged just twenty rupees for a consultation even in times of inflation. He never hesitated in referring some of his patients to specialists when required with letters of recommendation. He left no stone unturned to put his best foot forward, always.

With the kind of respect he commands, it wouldn't take him much to own a fancy place and charge huge fees. People would gladly pay, but then, that's just not him. The man truly lives up to Winston Churchill's words: 'We make a living by what we get, but we make a life by what we give.'

In a world consumed by greed and driven by materialism, there are still men like Dr K whose contribution to society is invaluable.

Raksha Raman

The Gift

My husband has been a practicing doctor for almost twenty-five years. Often, we receive cards and sweets from his patients who are about to get married or who have just had a baby. This time, he brought home a shopping bag.

'What's this?' I laughed when I saw it. It was some plain looking terry-cot material and was totally at variance with what I would normally buy.

Somewhat sheepishly, my husband told me that it was a gift from a patient's wife. He had seen the patient in the general ward of a public hospital a few days back. When he walked into the ward, there was quite a scene going on. The young man was comatose and surrounded by his weeping family. Some holy men had been called in and they were sprinkling Gangajal on him and saying prayers for his safe passage to the other world. Luckily, with proper medication, the man survived and went home.

A few days later, the man's wife came to the clinic with the bag. My husband thanked her and told her it was not necessary and that he didn't want it. But she insisted that he take it home for me. She said that she had stitched it with her own hands, especially for Doctor Saheb's wife.

On hearing this story, I looked at that ordinary bag with new eyes. I had received many gifts in my lifetime; I have received birthday cards, chocolates, dresses, trinkets and many more. But they had always been effortlessly bought in a shop. No one had ever made anything with their own hands. The woman must have given a thought to what I might need. She must have bought the material. Even if it cost her fifty or hundred bucks, it must have been a large percentage of her family's monthly income. It was as if someone had spent thousands of rupees on the material and then made the bag just for me.

Needless to say, this has been my favourite gift. I take it out every time I shop. It is environment friendly and it reminds me that it's always the thought behind the gift that counts.

Bhagyashree Sowani

The Unseen Doctor

A few years back my mother started complaining of back pain. Gradually the pain spread to her legs, making it difficult for her to walk. The doctor diagnosed it as a 'slip disc' and advised immediate surgery but my mother was unwilling. She sought the advice of her friends and relatives and started undergoing physiotherapy at a nearby hospital, hoping that would help her avoid the operation.

My father tried to convince her about the inevitability of surgery but without success. I lived in a different city and spoke to her on the phone for hours trying to do the same, but she refused to listen to a word I had to say.

The physiotherapy sessions did not help at all and to my mom's disappointment, she had to be hospitalised again. Mom was now under the care of a renowned and experienced orthopaedist, Dr Vaikar.

'Mrs Vasudeo, you need to get operated immediately. Have faith in me. Within two days of surgery, you would be able to walk, just like when you were young. Trust me, you are in safe hands,' Dr Vaikar patiently tried to convince my mother. To our great relief, she relented.

Unfortunately neither my pregnant sister nor I could fly down in time to be there during the surgery. Mom called me just before entering the operation theatre; she was crying and I held back my tears as I reassured her that everything would be fine.

After two hours, my father called and informed me that the surgery had been successful and Mom would regain consciousness in a few hours. It was a big respite to the family.

The next morning Mom called. 'Hi, beta, I'm perfectly fine. Don't worry about me.' Her cheerful voice put all my anxieties to rest. My mom was safe and free from all the pain she had suffered.

I haven't been able to meet the doctor who had worked this magic on my mother. All I know is that he made it possible for my mother to lead a comfortable and normal life, and I would always be thankful to him. It is no wonder why doctors are like God to us.

In order to express my gratitude to the doctor, I sent flowers and a 'thank you' card to his address, which I found through the hospital. I put my name, my identity (Mrs Vasudeo's daughter) and mobile number in the card. The next day I received an SMS from him which said, 'Most Welcome ... Take care of your mom ... Dr Vaikar'.

I have been in touch with him for four years now, sending him text messages on festivals and special occasions. And despite his busy schedules, each time, this gentleman of a doctor makes it a point to reply and acknowledge the wishes of an unknown and unseen person.

Komal Kudva

More Chicken Soup?

Share your heart with the rest of the world. If you have a story, poem or article (your own or someone else's) that you feel belongs in a future volume of Chicken Soup for the Indian Soul, please email us at cs.indiansoul@westland-tata.com or send it to:

Westland Ltd
S-35A, 3rd Floor
Green Park Main Market
New Delhi 110 016

We will make sure that you and the author are credited for the contribution. Thank you!

Contributors

Aarti K. Pathak is a professor of Economics, freelance writer, and travel enthusiast. Her writings have been published in several books and magazines. Contact her at aartikpat@gmail.com.

An MBA and software engineer, **Abhilasha Agarwal** likes to write poetry and fiction. She is a freelance graphic designer, who also works for the old and needy. Her writings have been published in vcherish.com, the *Statesman* and the *Times of India*. Her first ebook on poetry, *Vibrant Palette*, was published last year, and her poetry has been chosen for exhibition in the India Habitat Centre, New Delhi, by Jagori.

Aditi Gaur is a freelance writer. She has been contributing articles for online publication, and her first short story appeared in *Elle* magazine as a contest-winning entry in the October 2010 issue. She has also been guiding overseas high school students on the intricacies of essay writing. She can be reached at mona_gaur@hotmail.com.

Ajit is a practicing neuro physician.

Amrita Srinivasan is a consultant by profession and a writer by heart. Penning down life experiences and observations about human nature gives her immense satisfaction. She hopes to one day collate her experiences in the form of a novel. Contact her at c_amrita@yahoo.com.

Anil Jain is a cardiac surgeon who has recently gotten into farming. He can be reached at dranilrjain@gmai.com.

Anupama Kondayya is an analyst by profession, and a traveller, photographer, musician, theatre-artist and book-lover by passion. She is also a freelance writer and is foraying into play-writing as well. Based in Bangalore, she can be reached at anupamakondayya@gmail.com.

A freelance writer for many years, **Aparna Mathur** loves to write for children. She has earlier worked in a travel agency and an NGO for special children. She is also fond of singing. She can be reached at tanaymat@yahoo.co.in.

Archana Pande is a physiotherapist under training and a freelance writer for travel, lifestyle and business publications. Married to an IAF fighter pilot, she has lived and worked in various parts of India. She is an avid fitness enthusiast, blogger and nurtures a few bonsais.

Archna Pant is an ex-media and advertising professional. Currently a housewife, she is totally smitten with the kaleidoscope of life. Words are essential to her as they help her to reach out and connect. Contact her at archna22@hotmail.com.

Arti Sonthalia is a budding writer who writes from her soul. All her work is devoted to the lotus feet of her Guru who is her inspiration and guide. She can be contacted at 13artiag@gmail.com.

Avantika Debnath is just another girl with the ability to imagine. She sees a world full of people spreading joy and goodwill. As a writer, she believes every pleasant story should be shared with people. Those stories that do not have a pleasant end should be given an agreeable turn and left incomplete. She can be reached at avantika.debnath@gmail.com.

Bhagyashree Sowani lives with her dog in Ahmedabad. She likes travelling and trekking, and loves to watch movies over the weekend.

Bipasha Roy a PhD in Political Sociology and a degree in Law from Utkal University, Orissa. She has worked with the nautch girls of Kolkata and involved in the movement to eradicate ragging from the academic institutions of our country. She is also engaged in the reinducting 'out of school children' in schools and advocating for the rights of 'Child in

Conflict with Law'. She can be contacted at bipasha_roy5@rediffmail. com.

Deepak Morris is an author, playwright, stage director, stage actor and drama consultant, based in Pune. He has authored several guidebooks on managerial subjects and has written over two dozen musicals, plays and skits. Some of his plays have been performed in several countries, including South Africa, Wales, US and Canada. He can be reached at deepakmorris@rhapsodytheatre.org.

Deepika dreams of owning a cafe in the mountains. Then she rushes to earn a living. She's passionate about life, words, music, cooking, Darjeeling tea, and the Indian Railways. She is currently occupied trying to understand the finer nuances of human emotions and life. She can be reached at mencuckoo@gmail.com.

Ektaa G. Rupani is a wife, mother of two wonderful children, and a budding freelance writer. She has written for a few sites online and for the *Times of West Mumbai*. She also conducts creative writing and personality development workshops for children. She wishes to dedicate her writing to her dad, Late Shri Hari Narsinghani, who has always been her inspiration. She can be reached at rupani_ek@hotmail.com.

Gayathri Ponvannan is a network engineer and freelance writer. Her articles have been published in the *Gulf News,* the *Hindu*, *Chicken Soup for the Indian Soul* series, the *Christian Science Monitor* as well as in technical and HR management websites. She lives in Dubai with her husband and two sons, who along with her extended family in India take turns to be her muses. She can be reached at gayatripon@gmail.com.

Gunasekar Vuppalapati is a Consultant Plastic Surgeon at Apollo Hospitals and Clinical Director at GVG aesthetic health centre, Bangalore. He has received recognition for his work in plastic and aesthetic surgery, globally and has been featured in Who's Who in Medicine & Healthcare, published by Marquis Publication in USA. Gunasekar can be reached at doctor.guna@gmail.com.

Jane Bhandari coordinates 'Loquations', a Mumbai poetry-reading group, reviews poetry and children's books, and is co-editor of a forthcoming anthology of poetry for young people. She has published two volumes of poetry and two short story collections for children. She can be reached at janebhandari@yahoo.co.uk.

Joie Bose Chatterjee has degrees in Literature from St. Xaviers' College, Kolkata and JNU, New Delhi. Previously a freelance journalist and an educator, her creative endeavours have been published in newspapers and anthologies. Settled in Kolkata, she is now working on her collection of short stories and can be contacted at joiebose@gmail.com.

Jyoti Kerkar lives in Mumbai and is an avid reader. She likes to dabble in creative pursuits like painting, reading, music and craft. She believes writing just happened to her when the thoughts that crowded her mind found semblance on paper. She is also a tarot card reader. Contact her at jyotee9@gmail.com.

Kalaivani Asokan is a part-time teacher and a full-time homemaker with a passion for whipping up traditional dishes with a modern touch. At present she is busy compiling her favourite recipes, and hopes to bring out her cookery book soon. She can be reached at kalaionei@hotmail.com.

Komal Kudva works for an MNC, and office and routine household activities keep her busy during the week. However, on weekends she likes to pen down her stories and poems. Contact her at komal573@gmail.com.

Kunda Kagal writes articles and short stories for publications and magazines. She has worked for nearly twenty years as a visualiser-cum-copywriter in advertising agencies in Mumbai. She then started her own advertising agency called Shree Advertising Services, which she and her husband ran successfully for about fifteen years, after which she finally retired. She can be reached at kundakagal@gmail.com.

Leela Ramaswamy is an Honours graduate in English Literature from the University of Madras and B.Ed from the University of Bombay. She retired as a high school teacher. She writes regularly for the children's edition of a newspaper, and also contributes stories, features, poems and articles to various newspapers and magazines. She is the daughter of a doctor as well as the mother of one.

Lona is a doctor who enjoys writing.

Madhuri Jagadeesh has a Bachelor in Arts and a Masters in English Literature, and is a training and development consultant and singer/ songwriter with the world fusion band, MoonArra. She can be reached at moonarra@gmail.com.

Manish Chauhan is a mechanical engineer and M.Tech in Design of Mechanical Equipment from the Indian Institute of Technology, Delhi (2010 batch). He works as a researcher in the field of Robotics and is the author of a fictional book *RoCK-BEE* in the same domain. He can be reached at manishchauhan72@gmail.com.

Manjushree Abhinav is a film-maker cum novelist. *A Grasshopper's Pilgrimage* is the story of the love affair of a woman and a mountain. She also blogs at www.baktoo.blogspot.com, but is more alive and kicking on Facebook. If you are looking for someone who is radical and traditional at the same time, send her a friendship request. She blindly clicks 'yes' to all of them.

Manreet Sodhi Someshwar, a member of BlogAdda.com, is an award-winning writer and copywriter whose articles have featured in several publications including *New York Times*. She is the author of two novels: *Earning the Laundry Stripes* and *The Long Walk Home*. Visit her online at the-long-walk-home.blogspot.com.

Mita Banerjee has four decades of working as an educationist and a writer. She has recently re-started her old hobbies of stitching, knitting, crafting and embroidery with gusto. But what brings her greatest satisfaction is working with cancer patients by raising funds and cheering them up. She can be contacted at mitabaner@gmail.com.

N. Chokkan is a software consultant by profession, and trainer and author by interest. He works as a director for CRMIT Solutions Limited, Bangalore, leading its Training and Innovation divisions. He has authored many books of varied categories such as biographies, corporate histories, science and technology, self help etc. He lives in Bangalore with his wife, Uma, and two daughters Nangai and Mangai. He blogs at nagachokkanathan.wordpress.com and can be reached at nchokkan@ gmail.com.

Neebha Haribhakti is a practicing neuro-ophthalmologist (a rare branch of ophthalmology which deals with disorders of the optic nerve, brain and spine) for the past five years in Ahmedabad. A poet, music lover, avid reader and traveller, she has a passion for designing.

Neelam Chandra is an officer with Indian Railways. About a hundred of her stories and poems and two of her books have been published. She won second prize in a competition organized by Pratham Books and one of her stories won an award in a contest organized by the Children's Book Trust in 2009. She has also been awarded the second prize by Gulzar in a poetry contest organised by the American Society. She can be reached at neelamsaxena27@yahoo.com.

Nikita Pancholi is currently in college and lives in Delhi.

Pranit Paras is an eager reader, an aspiring writer and believes in living life on his own terms. He is a nature lover, and passionate about movies, cricket and basket ball. He can be reached at www.paramabhas.blogspot. com.

Prerna Shah believes in the magic of a well-told story. For seven-and-a-half years, she wrote stories for a newspaper. Then she went on to pursue a second masters in Creative and Life Writing at Goldsmiths, University of London. If you have an interesting story to share, she would love to hear from you at write2prerna@gmail.com.

Raamesh Gowri Raghavan moonlights as a copywriter by day and as a poet and writer by night. He thinks he writes really funny stuff, but his friends don't seem to agree. His dearest wish is to be remembered with tears a century after his time.

Rajivi Prabhakar Rao is a twenty-one-year-old advertising graduate with a passion for writing poetry and stories. She believes in second chances and creating opportunities for herself. She also believes that people must always accept and love themselves because in the end, it's what happens in one's life that eventually shapes them into who they are today. She can be reached at rajivirao@gmail.com.

Raksha Raman, a member of BlogAdda.com is an ex-investment banker and now an aspiring novelist. She is an avid blogger who writes about various topics she feels strongly about. Apart from weaving stories and penning poems, she is also a music and travel enthusiast, and can be reached at raksha.raman@gmail.com.

Ramya Nisal is a general surgeon, and along with her plastic surgeon husband, runs a surgical hospital in Nagpur. Ramya is a voracious reader and also loves to write whenever her demanding career and her two teenage kids allow the time for it. She can be reached at ramyanisal@gmail.com.

Rashmi Balakrishnan is based in Bangalore. She enjoys reading, listening to ghazals and dancing. She can be reached at letustalk.rashmi@gmail.com.

Ratnadip Acharya is a well-trained street magician. He lives in Mumbai where he works as an electrical engineer for a living. He travels extensively, and many of his stories have been published in different titles of the Chicken Soup series. Contact him at ratnadip76@gmail.com.

Ravindranath Sharma is enjoying his retired life with his grandchildren and catching up on reading. His all-time favourite reads include Hercule Poirot mysteries and the *Chicken Soup for the Soul* series. He can be reached at rn42sharma@rediffmail.com.

Reeta Mani is a virologist at the National Institute of Mental Health and Neurosciences (NIMHANS), Bangalore. She can be reached at drreeta@gmail.com.

Rehana Ali is a school teacher by choice. She gave up a career in cytogenetics to teach school children, a decision she has never regretted. She is also an environmentalist who enjoys trekking and nature excursions with her school children and is an aspiring writer. She can be reached at ali.rehana@gmail.com.

Reshmi Kurup, a member of BlogAdda.com, is a young blogger from Mumbai who loves to travel, read and write about the world. Blogging is not just writing for her but the means to convey her thoughts to her fellow survivors in this world. She can be reached at writetorevathi@gmail.com.

Revathi Seshadri lives in Nagpur. She loves animals and reading books, and her keyboard that obliges the one-finger typist when she is possessed by the muse. A few of her stories have appeared in some of the Chicken Soup series. Of late, she has taken a fancy for writing short stories and is testing the waters. Reach her at revathi.seshadri@gmail.com.

Roshan Radhakrishnan, a member of BlogAdda.com, is an anaesthesiologist from Kannur in Kerala, presently working in Mangalore. He is an eclectic combination of an insatiable foodie, a trusted friend and an absent-minded professor. An Aquarian and a dog lover, he is an avid blogger. He loves how the written word helps unite people irrespective of culture, caste and religion. He can be reached at pythoroshan@gmail.com.

Rugvedita Satyajeet Parakh is a consultant oncopathologist. Her work has been recognised with an excellence award in 2010 for the bladder cancer research by the International Society of Urologic Pathology (ISUP), at Washington, DC during USCAP. She enjoys writing and editing for Pathologyonline.com, theatre and dramatics. An important aspect of her life is family — her husband and a three year old. She can be reached at rugvedita.parakh@gmail.com.

Sangeetha P. Sukumar is a diabetologist working in the Amrita Institute of Medical Sciences, Kochi, Kerala. She can be reached at sangeethapsukumar@aims.amrita.edu.

A consultant, **Sanjeev Trivedi** works with people to help them realise their career/business and other goals in life. In the last twenty-nine years he has transformed the lives of many, while working with corporates, business houses, hospitals and educational institutions. He is an acclaimed motivational trainer and also an astrologer. Contact: trivedisanjeev@gmail.com.

Saurabh Paul loves reading novels, particularly classics and autobiographies, and loves to share the experiences that have left a lasting impact on him. He loves playing table tennis, cricket and the tabla. He can be reached at paul.saurabh@gmail.com.

Savitri Babulkar is a retired teacher and freelance journalist. Her hobbies include reading, writing, music and dramatics. She can be reached at savitri.babulkar@gmail.com.

Shashi Agarwal is a homemaker and mother of two daughters. She likes a bit of both reading and writing. She can be reached at agarwalsash@gmail.com.

Sheela Jaywant writes because she likes to. Columnist, author and translator, she has written *Quilted, Melting Moments, The Liftman and Other Stories*, and some non-fiction books as well. Her stories have won prizes in several competitions and one story, 'Relocation' was included in *Vanilla Desires*, an anthology of short stories. Her stories have featured in the Chicken Soup series. Her email: sheelajaywant@yahoo.co.in.

Shifa Maitra loves carrying tales and carries them inside her head all the time. Writing is something she has to do! That's not what she does for a living; it's what she does for life. She has written TV shows, live events, title tracks for TV shows, songs for a feature film and stories for the Chicken Soup series. She is a creative director at UTV Bindass and can be contacted at shifamaitra@gmail.com.

Shreeja Mohatta Jhawar is a web and graphics designer and event manager under the banner of Think Unlike Creative Cocoon. She is also a writer and a philanthropist who runs a volunteer group 'Kritagya' aiming to serve the old and derelict. For her, writing is reflecting. She has a spiritual and liberal approach. She can be reached at shreeja.jhawar@gmail.com.

Shreya Jain is a twelve-year-old student of grade seven studying in Gurgaon. Apart from writing, she enjoys reading, drawing and playing the keyboard. She is a member of the basketball and soccer team and loves her pet guinea pig, Coco. Greatly inspired by her uncle, she hopes to become a doctor one day and travel across the world. Contact: shreyajain98@hotmail.com.

Shubhada Sanjay Khirwadkar is a practicing child specialist and child counsellor based in Nagpur. She can be reached at shubha.khirwadkar@gmail.com.

Smita Shenoy is a freelance writer and an untrained teacher. She is a voracious reader and spends her free time buried in a book or a magazine. Of course, free time is a rare commodity as her two kids tend to keep her on her toes. She can be reached at smitasshenoy@gmail.com.

Sonal Saxena is Professor, Dept of Microbiology, Lady Hardinge Medical College, New Delhi. She is married to an engineer and has a twelve-year-old daughter. She loves to read, write, teach and cook, and can be reached at sonalsaxena3@rediffmail.com.

Sucheta Tiwari is a final year medical student from New Delhi. She's a self confessed nerd and bookworm who loves to write. She loves to travel too but medicine tops the list of the things she likes. She is also a regular blogger and can be reached at her blog, 'Diary of a Sleepy Kid', sleepykidlivingadream.blogspot.com or at sucheta.tiwari@gmail.com.

Sue Ghosh is a journalist and aspiring novelist. She can be reached at sud24@hotmail.com.

Sunil Choudhary is Director of Max Institute of Aesthetic & Reconstructive Surgery, Max Healthcare, Delhi. He was previously a consultant plastic surgeon in the National Health Service of UK. He was recently chosen as the country's best reconstructive surgeon by *Brunch* magazine, published by *Hindustan Times*. Reach him at sunil.choudhary@maxhealthcare.com.

Sunita Maheshwari is a Senior Paediatric Cardiologist and also the Chief Dreamer of Teleradiology Solutions (www.telradsol.com) and RXDX. She is active in the social arena where she runs two trust funds: People4people, which puts up playgrounds in poorer sections of Karnataka, and Telrad Foundation that provides low-cost high-quality diagnostics to rural areas of India. She can be reached at sunita.maheshwari@telradsol.com.

Sutirtha Saha is an MNC-employed computer engineer, living in Hyderabad. He loves writing short stories and has won awards for his writings. He has contributed to quite a few Chicken soup compilations. He can be reached at sutirtha.saha@gmail.com.

Swati Rajgarhia is a writer/editor by day, a reader by night and a mom 24/7. She dreams of giving tangibility to her thoughts one day in the shape of a book. She can be reached at swatirajgarhia@yahoo.com.

T.S. Karthik has an MBA from the Indian Institute of Planning and Management, Chennai. He is a voracious reader, an aspiring writer, and has won several prizes in business quizzes. His pastime includes watching movies, plays and listening to music. He believes in inspiring and motivating people to achieve their dreams. He can be reached at tskarthik13@yahoo.com.

Tulika Mukerjee Saha writes as a hobby. She has written several poems, short stories and has also co-authored a series of English textbooks. She is an avid reader and is a teacher by profession. She tries to encourage her students to express themselves through prose or poetry. She can be reached at tulikasaha@gmail.com.

Upreet Dhaliwal, an ophthalmologist by profession, is an avid reader of romantic fiction. However, given her hectic lifestyle that includes patient care, and parenting, she can rarely be self-indulgent. Blogging is a recent passion and she can be found on Sulekha.com, where she uses the nom-de-plume 'Seeing Eye'. She can be reached at upreetdhaliwal@yahoo.com.

Vandana Vij can be reached at vijvandana@rediffmail.com.

Vibhuti Bhandarkar, a member of BlogAdda.com, is a qualified graphic designer and copywriter working for over five years in the advertising industry in Pune. She has also contributed to The Times of India bi-weekly supplements – Eastside Plus & Westside Plus, Pune. A passionate and prolific blogger, she will debut as a published author soon with her collection of short stories later this year. She can be reached at vibhuti.bb@gmail.com.

Vijay Fulchand Parakh is a retired dentist who practiced and resides at a humble town in southern Maharashtra, Ichalkaranji. He graduated from Government Dental College, Mumbai.. He comes from the family of freedom fighters and is originally from Igatpuri. He is an avid reader, thinker and philosopher. He is blessed with a wife, a son and a daughter. He loves spending his time with his granddaughters. He can be reached at +91-230-2430474.

Vivek Banerjee is a paediatrician in real life and a writer in his dreams. His début novel, *The Long Road*, published in January 2011 has received a favourable response. He blogs at drvbanerjee.blogspot.com and may be contacted at drvbanerjee@hotmail.com.

Zainab Sulaiman is a freelance writer and businesswoman – she makes children's quilts under the Fatcat label and is a busy mother to two young children. She writes a blog on the simple joys, challenges and rewards of parenting at www.memoriesofchocolate.wordpress.com and can be reached at fatcatbangalore@yahoo.com.

Permissions

Matter of Life and Death. Reprinted by permission of Shashi Agarwal. © 2011 Shashi Agarwal.

The Doctor of Champawat. Reprinted by permission of Archna Pant. © 2011 Archna Pant.

The Pact. Reprinted by permission of Ajit. © 2011 Ajit.

Amma and Doctor Uttam. Reprinted by permission of *Rehana Ali.* © 2011 Rehana Ali.

Being a Chocolate Boy. Reprinted by permission of Sue Ghosh. © 2011 Sue Ghosh.

Both a Mother and a Doctor. Reprinted by permission of Gayathri Ponvannan. © 2011 Gayathri Ponvannan.

Doctor Babu. Reprinted by permission of Avantika Debnath. © 2011 Avantika Debnath.

Dr Santa. Reprinted by permission of Swati Rajgharia. © 2011 Swati Rajgharia.

Ria's Birthday. Reprinted by permission of Sheela Jaywant. © 2011 Sheela Jaywant.

Erased. Reprinted by permission of Shubhada Sanjay Khirwadkar. © 2011 Shubhada Sanjay Khirwadkar.

Special Bonds. Reprinted by permission of Archana Pande. © 2011 Archana Pande.

The Magic Potion. Reprinted by permission of Smita Shenoy. © 2011 Smita Shenoy.

The Silent Thief. Reprinted by permission of Arti Sonthalia. © 2011 Arti Sonthalia.

The Extra Mile. Reprinted by permission of Swati Rajgharia. © 2011 Swati Rajgharia.

A Mentor in Need. Reprinted by permission of Smita Shenoy. © 2011 Smita Shenoy.

Birth on the Berth of a Train. Reprinted by permission of Jyoti Kerkar. © 2011 Jyoti Kerkar.

Docs Don't Cry. Reprinted by permission of Sutirtha Saha. © 2011 Sutirtha Saha.

Lateral Thinking. Reprinted by permission of T.S. Karthik. © 2011 T.S. Karthik.

Touched By an Angel. Reprinted by permission of Joie Bose Chatterjee. © 2011 Joie Bose Chatterjee.

A Piece of Bread. Reprinted by permission of Anil Jain. © 2011 Anil Jain.

Anywhere at All. Reprinted by permission of Sheela Jaywant. © 2011 Sheela Jaywant.

Doctor of Hearts. Reprinted by permission of Kunda Kagal. © 2011 Kunda Kagal.

Doctored. Reprinted by permission of Madhuri Jagadeesh. © 2011 Madhuri Jagadeesh.

Magical Hands. Reprinted by permission of Arti Sonthalia. © 2011 Arti Sonthalia.

The Letters. Reprinted by permission of Gayathri Ponvannan. © 2011 Gayathri Ponvannan.

The Other Side. Reprinted by permission of Vivek Banerjee. © 2011 Vivek Banerjee.

An Eye for an Eye. Reprinted by permission of Sucheta Tiwari. © 2011 Sucheta Tiwari.

Doctors in Bed. Reprinted by permission of Sheela Jaywant. © 2011 Sheela Jaywant.

He Taught Me Trust. Reprinted by permission of Shreeja Mohatta Jhawar. © 2011 Shreeja Mohatta Jhawar.

His Miracle. Reprinted by permission of Sangeetha P. Sukumar. © 2011 Sangeetha P. Sukumar.

Indelible. Reprinted by permission of Shreya Jain. © 2011 Shreya Jain.

Of Compassion and Empathy. Reprinted by permission of Deepika. © 2011 Deepika.

Selfless Love. Reprinted by permission of Sonal Saxena. © 2011 Sonal Saxena.

The True Healer. Reprinted by permission of Leela Ramaswamy. © 2011 Leela Ramaswamy.

Two-minute Consultation. Reprinted by permission of Sunita Maheshwari. © 2011 Sunita Maheshwari.

When Patients are Teachers. Reprinted by permission of Sheela Jaywant. © 2011 Sheela Jaywant.

Words from a Stranger. Reprinted by permission of Nikita Pancholi. © 2011 Nikita Pancholi.

A Job Well Done. Reprinted by permission of Tulika Mukerjee Saha. © 2011 Tulika Mukerjee Saha.

Beyond Our Understanding. Reprinted by permission of Sunita Maheshwari. © 2011 Sunita Maheshwari.

Every Day Holds the Possibility of a Miracle. Reprinted by permission of Sunil Choudhary. © 2011 Sunil Choudhary.

From the Diary of Dr Biswas. Reprinted by permission of Ratnadip Acharya. © 2011 Ratnadip Acharya.

A Brush with Doctors. Reprinted by permission of Lona. © 2011 Lona.

A Clinic with No Patients. Reprinted by permission of N. Chokkan. © 2011 N. Chokkan.

A Unique Patient. Reprinted by permission of Vijay Parakh. © 2011 Vijay Parakh.

Black Magic. Reprinted by permission of Manish Chauhan. © 2011 Manish Chauhan.

Mommy's 'Hungry Baby' Syndrome. Reprinted by permission of Prerna Shah. © 2011 Prerna Shah.

Saviour. Reprinted by permission of Sanjeev Trivedi. © 2011 Sanjeev Trivedi.

The Circus of Life. Reprinted by permission of Aditi Gaur. © 2011 Aditi Gaur.

The Doctor Who Got Chicken Spots. Reprinted by permission of Jane Bhandari. © 2011 Jane Bhandari.

The Lighter Moments of Medicine. Reprinted by permission of Ramya Nisal. © 2011 Ramya Nisal.

A Lifetime of Living. Reprinted by permission of Bhagyashree Sowani. © 2011 Bhagyashree Sowani.

Communicate. Reprinted by permission of Upreet Dhaliwal. © 2011 Upreet Dhaliwal.

From the Wallet. Reprinted by permission of Sheela Jaywant. © 2011 Sheela Jaywant.

Humility: The Hallmark of Greatness. Reprinted by permission of Kalaivani Asokan. © 2011 Kalaivani Asokan.

India Has It. Reprinted by permission of Manjushree Abhinav. © 2011 Manjushree Abhinav.

Pain in the Neck. Reprinted by permission of Ravindranath Sharma. © 2011 Ravindranath Sharma.

The ICU. Reprinted by permission of Deepak Morris. © 2011 Deepak Morris.

Circa 1988. Reprinted by permission of Chandramohan Asrani. © 2011 Chandramohan Asrani.

Lady Saviour. Reprinted by permission of Reshmi Kurup. © 2011 Reshmi Kurup.

One Last Visit. Reprinted by permission of Saurabh Paul. © 2011 Saurabh Paul.

The Escape. Reprinted by permission of Vibhuti Bhandarkar. © 2011 Vibhuti Bhandarkar.

The God Complex. Reprinted by permission of Roshan Radhakrishnan. © 2011 Roshan Radhakrishnan.

A Cup of Milk. Reprinted by permission of Bipasha Roy. © 2011 Bipasha Roy.

A Doctor's Legacy. Reprinted by permission of Prerna Shah. © 2011 Prerna Shah.

An Early Diagnosis. Reprinted by permission of Mita Banerjee. © 2011 Mita Banerjee.

Doctor Do-Little Versus Doctor Do-a-Lot. Reprinted by permission of Zainab Sulaiman. © 2011 Zainab Sulaiman.

Knowledge Shield. Reprinted by permission of Sanjeev Trivedi. © 2011 Sanjeev Trivedi.

My Wonderful Vaidya. Reprinted by permission of Anupama Kondayya. © 2011 Anupama Kondayya.

The Doctor on Green Street. Reprinted by permission of Savitri Babulkar. © 2011 Savitri Babulkar.

The Flip Side. Reprinted by permission of Ektaa Rupani. © 2011 Ektaa Rupani.

The Philosopher Who Cares. Reprinted by permission of Jane Bhandari. © 2011 Jane Bhandari.

The Stitch. Reprinted by permission of Pranit Paras. © 2011 Pranit Paras.

A Homeopathic Experience. Reprinted by permission of Manjushree Abhinav. © 2011 Manjushree Abhinav.

A Hug. Reprinted by permission of Rashmi Balakrishnan . © 2011 Rashmi Balakrishnan .

Musical Touch. Reprinted by permission of Deepika. © 2011 Deepika.

The Healing Process. Reprinted by permission of Kalaivani Asokan. © 2011 Kalaivani Asokan.

The Power of Belief. Reprinted by permission of Abhilasha Agarwal. © 2011 Abhilasha Agarwal.

The Subtle Art of Healing. Reprinted by permission of Sanjeev Trivedi. © 2011 Sanjeev Trivedi.

The Wrong Right. Reprinted by permission of Reeta Mani. © 2011 Reeta Mani.

Trading in Hope. Reprinted by permission of Shifa Maitra. © 2011 Shifa Maitra.

A Doctor Bows Down. Reprinted by permission of Shashi Agarwal. © 2011 Shashi Agarwal.

Doctor Joshi. Reprinted by permission of Neelam Chandra. © 2011 Neelam Chandra.

Faith – I Take a Bow! Reprinted by permission of Deepika. © 2011 Deepika.

A Doctor's Dream. Reprinted by permission of Rajivi Prabhakar Rao. © 2011 Rajivi Prabhakar Rao.

Never Give Up. Reprinted by permission of Sunita Maheshwari. © 2011 Sunita Maheshwari.

Restoring Faith. Reprinted by permission of Rugvedita Parakh. © 2011 Rugvedita Parakh.

The Book. Reprinted by permission of Amrita Srinivasan. © 2011 Amrita Srinivasan.

The Dream. Reprinted by permission of Aparna Mathur. © 2011 Aparna Mathur.

A Chapati of Jowar. Reprinted by permission of Neebha Haribhakti. © 2011 Neebha Haribhakti.

Change. Reprinted by permission of Raamesh Gowri Raghavan. © 2011 Raamesh Gowri Raghavan.

In the Best Hands. Reprinted by permission of Vandana Vij. © 2011 Vandana Vij.

Colours of Darkness. Reprinted by permission of Avantika Debnath. © 2011 Avantika Debnath.

Crossroads. Reprinted by permission of Manreet Sodhi Someshwar. © 2011 Manreet Sodhi Someshwar.

It Worked Both Ways. Reprinted by permission of Revathi Seshadri. © 2011 Revathi Seshadri.

Some More Time. Reprinted by permission of Sunita Maheswari. © 2011 Sunita Maheswari.

Thank you, Dr K! Reprinted by permission of Raksha Raman. © 2011 Raksha Raman.

The Gift. Reprinted by permission of Bhagyashree Sowani. © 2011 Bhagyashree Sowani.

The Unseen Doctor. Reprinted by permission of Komal Kudva. © 2011 Komal Kudva.

Konark Challun

22-9-11

westland